my 180

trusting God more

John Covach

Knowing Who Walks Beside You

NORTHWESTERN PUBLISHING HOUSE
Milwaukee, Wisconsin

All Scripture quotations, unless otherwise indicated, are taken from the Holy Bible, New International Version®, NIV®. Copyright © 1973, 1978, 1984, 2011 by Biblica, Inc.™ Used by permission of Zondervan. All rights reserved worldwide. www.zondervan.com.

The "NIV" and "New International Version" are trademarks registered in the United States Patent and Trademark Office by Biblica, Inc.™

All hymns, unless otherwise indicated, are taken from *Christian Worship: Hymnal*. © 2021 by Northwestern Publishing House.

All rights reserved. This publication may not be copied, photocopied, reproduced, translated, or converted to any electronic or machine-readable form in whole or in part, except for brief quotations, without prior written approval from the publisher.

Northwestern Publishing House
N16W23379 Stone Ridge Dr. Waukesha, WI 53188
www.nph.net
© 2025 Northwestern Publishing House
Published 2025
Printed in the United States of America
ISBN 978-0-8100-2937-8
ISBN 978-0-8100-2938-5 (e-book)

Foreword

What if you were challenged to dedicate yourself to a specific pattern of thinking during a certain number of days and under definite spiritual disciplines? Would you accept the experiment?

That's exactly what happened for several people who were invited not just to touch on a study topic like seeking God more or loving God more. They were to devote themselves to a full 180 days of reading about that topic in the Bible itself, praying about the topic for themselves, journaling their adventure, and even engaging an accountability partner to help them stick to the commitment and to talk through the details they were discovering. After that, they were to share what they learned about the topic with you.

You are looking at the results of one of the challenges.

And you're in for quite a journey. Whether you read this by yourself, in a small group of fellow inquirers, or in another setting, you will gain tremendous insights from reading what this author learned.

Do you have to do your own 180? Won't that first take a lot of Scripture knowledge? No, not at all. But if you do take up the challenge for yourself, there's no telling the spiritual growth you'll experience. After 180 days of reading and considering God's own Word on a spiritual topic, your Savior promises rich dividends. "Consider carefully what you hear," he says in Mark 4:24. "With the measure you use, it will be measured to you—and even more." You will certainly discover rich understanding. You may even experience a complete turnaround in your life with Jesus!

Now read what happened when John Covach accepted the challenge.

Contents

Prologue

1. Finding Your Starting Point 1
2. The Daily Routine. 5
3. Our Journey's Destination 21
4. Family: Looking Back at the Road Already Traveled 35
5. Friends: Helping Those Who Travel With Us 47
6. Promises Kept: Trusting God With the Road Ahead 59
7. Check Engine: Repentance Led by Trust. 71
8. Driving Forward: A Harvest Fueled by Trust. 83
9. Giving Directions: Pointing Others to the Way Ahead 93
10. The Road to More Trust Doesn't Need to Be Lonely 107
11. A Journey With Miraculous Expectations. 119
12. Destination Ahead: Trusting Through Life's End 129
13. The Journey Continues. 139

Prologue

"I do believe; help me overcome my unbelief!" (Mark 9:24). It is a paradox: two true statements that seem to contradict each other, yet both remain true. "I do believe!" The man who said this did trust in Jesus! After all, hadn't he come to the miracle worker for a miracle cure? But he also had his doubts.

The dilemma involved his son, a boy tormented by an "impure spirit" (Mark 9:25). Imagine: The devil had sent one of his hellish henchmen to rob the boy of his ability to speak. Worse than that, the same child had been gripped by seizures since childhood. Add to the desperation that Jesus' disciples were powerless to save the child. And it was public. A crowd rushed to the scene. Had they come to help? Or to witness the spectacle of the hopeless?

This situation was bad. Often the demon had thrown the boy into fire or water to kill the child. Do you get where this father was coming from? Do you understand the desperation he has for his child? He pleads with Jesus because he trusts the Lord can help. But right beside faith were nagging questions and, if the truth be told . . . unbelief.

I agreed to the My 180 project because the words of this father can come from my mouth: "O Lord Jesus, I believe. Thanks to you, I trust, but . . . " Does a "but" negate everything confessed before it? Not necessarily. Can faith and no faith, trust and no trust, live in the same heart? They do. Right beside my confidence in the Lord, there is a shade of doubt. A hint of fear. A little worry . . . or, in fact, a pile of the stuff that keeps me anxious. I trust yet see what seems to be an impossible situation. I panic. I count the obstacles. I go negative and believe something else: "No one can help; nothing can be done; it's another hopeless cause."

I believe in my Savior, though. I do trust God. However, life, the sin in me, and, yes, a real devil work to wear my faith down or tear it to shreds. I need increased faith. More faith. Growing faith. The man with the demon-possessed son asked Jesus for more than healing. Part of the plea was "Help me overcome my unbelief!"

So, why read this? Why spend 180 days in your life in the pursuit of trusting God more? I don't have to answer the question *why* for you. You opened this book because you know why. You need something. You need more.

Maybe you have just begun your journey with Jesus. You need to learn more and to trust Jesus in a greater way. Maybe you are at a spiritual low. You understand that you are not a faith-filled, "faith-full" child of God. The needle on your trust gauge is buried deep on empty. Maybe you walked away from the Lord and need to come back. You remember days when you and Jesus were *hold two fingers tightly together* close. Now it frightens you to think how far you have drifted from his side. Maybe you believe your church let you down. Maybe it did. This has shaken your confidence in the church and your trust in God. Maybe you need miracles in your life. Come on, who couldn't use a miracle?! And the miracle you're praying for? "It's my health." "My relationships." "My money." "My marriage." "My children." "My country." "My church." And the trust left in your heart is urging, "Go to Jesus. Ask for his help!"

In Mark chapter 9, you can read about what happened to the troubled boy with the equally troubled father. Expect the unexpected! Welcome to your 180. Jesus said, "Everything is possible for one who believes" (Mark 9:23)!

> **Note:** *Some chapters of this book deal with difficult subjects such as physical and sexual abuse, abortion, and suicide. If any of these difficult subjects are covered in a chapter, a note will follow that chapter title to alert the reader.*

Finding Your Starting Point

How do you begin? It has been a little over a year since I asked this very question. I was invited to do a "180" and I thought, "Why not?" If I hadn't been asked, I probably wouldn't have thought of it on my own. My trust in the Lord was not at a low ebb. I was not in a crisis. I'm retired! You know, the "every day is Saturday" set. I have a devotional life. Up till now, I've been given trust enough to get to . . . now.

Imagine me at a support group for people who want to learn to trust God more. By the way, they have that—it is called church. I'd say, "Hi, my name is John, and I'm a believer. I can't remember a time I wasn't aware of God or didn't feel a need to depend on God. I was born in a snowstorm on Christmas Day and born again into God's family by the start of the new year. A television evangelist says that makes me a 'lifer'! My first memories include prayers to God and Bible stories about our great God. Most everything in school was hard for me: catching a baseball, cutting with scissors, reading, doing math, making friends. God, on the other hand, was my best subject."

Little Johnny couldn't wait to get to Sunday school. Don't confuse this with behaving in Sunday school. I was the naughtiest kid in class but literally heard and remembered everything my exasperated teacher taught. I attended a private, Christian elementary school. I had a C in arithmetic, a C in spelling, a D in behavior, and an A in Word of God. I went to a Christian high school (Go, MLS Cardinals!), a Christian college, and a

Christian graduate school. The grades in my classes got better. And God was still my major.

I have faith for today. However, I recognize that I have no idea what tomorrow may bring. Every day, new challenges test trust. So having a trust in the Lord that grows and matures to face tomorrow is a good idea, and, by the way, that growing, maturing trust is God's will for me . . . and for you.

I believe in the God who reveals himself in the Bible. Maybe you are coming from the same place. Or maybe you had a different starting point but are now looking to the Bible for answers. How did you first meet the three-in-one God revealed in Scripture?

Maybe you were like Timothy of long ago. His mother and grandmother were devout Christians. From infancy they taught the boy about his Savior. St. Paul the apostle said the same faith that lived in them was passed to the child they loved (2 Timothy 1:5; 3:14-16). Did you have parents, or a parent or grandparent, who made certain you knew the God who died for you on the cross? I did. My mother nurtured her husband and four children in trusting God more. I remember sitting in the big chair with Mom and *The Bible in Pictures*. She taught me about Jesus' love for a lifetime of hope. Did you have a family member who did that for you?

Maybe a stranger told you about our saving God. I was a door-to-door evangelist for five years. Some of the conversations from those experiences make my life very rich. Like the story of Philip and the Ethiopian (Acts 8:26-39), your story of faith could be a journey of trust involving a puzzled heart, a helpful stranger, and an introduction to your Lord.

Did you meet Jesus in a class or with a worship group? Crowds came to learn from Jesus at the seashore or on the grassy hills and left as trusting disciples. Sometimes friends invited others to come and see what Jesus could say and do (John 1:29-42). Those meetings left some forever changed in their attitude toward Christ. Think back—is this how it worked for you? Who do you need to thank? For me personally, I need to say thank you to Edgar Hoenecke, Norm Berg, Leonard Koeninger,

Jim Fricke, John Jeske, Dick Winters, and J. P. Meyer. Most of these friends to my faith are in heaven already. Jesus will pass on my gratitude to them. And to the rest I say, "Thank you." Each, in his own way, led me in the right direction at a time when I needed to trust more.

No matter how you met Christ, there was always a common denominator: the promises of God connected to a conversation, an activity, or class touched your mind and heart. St. Paul puts it this way: "Faith comes from hearing the message, and the message is heard through the word about Christ" (Romans 10:17). God speaks through his Word in the Bible. God creates trust (faith) in what he says as we listen to what he says and see it fulfilled, just as he says. Do you desire more trust? Keep going to the source and receive the blessing.

As you begin this journey of trusting the Lord more and more, it is vitally important you remember this promise from Romans 10:17. I find that we are willing to read what others say about trust while overlooking the real power that creates trust.

You could google *trusting* and may get a bit of good information along with some bad. You could drag out a dictionary, thesaurus, and encyclopedia and search *faith*, *believing*, and *trust*. You could listen to Christian music and watch inspirational movies about faith or read books on Christian teaching that outline and explain all that the Bible says about trusting. In fact, I encourage you to do just that. But don't stop there. Paul also said in Romans, "I am not ashamed of the gospel, because it is the power of God that brings salvation to everyone who believes" (Romans 1:16). The dynamic power that saves by igniting and fueling trust in the Savior is the gospel, the good news of the Bible. Make going to the Bible, the source of all trust in God, a lifelong pursuit.

The Daily Routine

I'm ready now to share how my 180 worked.

Begin with prayer. Starting day 1, and every day of my 180, I began with prayer. I didn't rush to get through a quick conversation with God. It wasn't a requirement. It was a plea, an earnest request for our God's blessing. I reminded God that he asked me to pray fearlessly, persistently, and expectantly for his gifts (Luke 11:5-13). God promises that he will hear and answer prayers for the Spirit's blessing with a big "Yes!" (Luke 11:13). The Holy Spirit will work in you to create and increase your trust in God (1 Corinthians 12:3). So, ask for the heavenly Father's blessing and the Holy Spirit's gift. Expect the Holy Spirit to lead you into God's Word.

Choose your resources. My 180 is a dedicated time for spiritual study. If this puts you off from the start, you are short-circuiting your own spiritual growth. I could have read many books written by fascinating Christian authors. I hesitated to do that. Instead, I continued my daily and weekly routine of devotions and worship: I sip my first cup of coffee each morning reading *Meditations*, a daily devotional from Northwestern Publishing House. It has a theme for each week with a Bible passage assigned and applied to each day. I follow that with a second cup of coffee and my *Grace Moments* from Time of Grace Ministries, another daily devotional with practical application from God's Word. On Sunday morning, I set the alarm an hour early and tune in to worship with *Time of Grace* on my television. It helps me prepare myself for a morning of worship, which includes a service at my local church. I hear Bible readings, hymns with strong Bible lyrics, and sermons that help me see how God's Word is speaking to my life.

Read the Scriptures. Most important, my 180 took me directly to the Bible. I've been a Bible reader most of my life. I helped my children and wife read through the entire Bible multiple times in our morning devotions. But the time I set aside for my 180 was different. This was not done primarily for others. This careful reading was for me, for God to answer my prayer to trust him more!

I started my journey in the historic books of the Old Testament, and from there I went to the gospels. I took it slow. Scripture encourages us to meditate on God's Word. Not to clear our minds to emptiness but to fill our minds by contemplating the words and thoughts of the Bible. Think about what each verse of Scripture is saying to you. Don't rush this. We are in a spiritual marathon, not a hundred-yard dash.

Then, later in my journey, I read whole books of the Bible the way they were intended to be read. Books like Galatians, Titus, or Philemon are letters to believers, so I read them like you would read a letter: from start to finish. I looked for big themes that wrapped themselves around individual chapters and verses. If you have not done this, expect a treat. You won't just get stuck on a tree but will really get the big picture and see the beauty of the forest.

Take time to journal. To help with this slow and methodical study, I kept a handwritten journal of my 180. I encourage you to chronicle your own study, your Bible discoveries, and what is happening in your personal life each day of the experiment. Buy a spiral-bound notebook or set up a journal page on your electronic device—some place where it will be easy to write your thoughts as they come to you.

With each Bible reading, I asked the four "W's" (who, what, where, and when) to help me stay aware of context and identify the general message of each section. It matters whether Moses said something, prophets said it hundreds of years before the first Christmas, Jesus is teaching, or the apostles are talking to the church. But don't stop there. Here are four more questions to help you journal:

- What does this reading teach me about God?
- What does this reading teach me about sin?
- What does this reading teach me about God's love and forgiveness in Christ Jesus?
- And finally, how does this reading help me with trusting God more?

There may not be detailed answers to each of these questions in each reading. On some days it may be difficult for you to see Jesus in the reading, especially in the Old Testament. It is okay. Each chapter of this book will have some study points for you to focus on as I share thoughts with you in the sections marked "From My Journal." I share with you parts of my journaling journey as I invite you to journal along with me. Above all, do your best to see, to listen, and to ask God to help you trust him more as we study together.

TIPS ALONG THE WAY

- **Make the time.** This is important. Please don't cheat by cutting out part of your 180: prayer, Bible reading, and reflection in your journal. The time you spend doing these things is a quiet time for you and God. It's just you and your Lord every day or as often as you choose to pursue your experiment. I'm a slow reader. For me, this meant an hour to an hour and a half of quiet time with God.

- **Pick your study space.** The place was wherever I happened to be. Most often my journal, Bible, and pen were sitting on my kitchen table. This was also a gentle reminder to follow my 180 every time I went to the refrigerator. However, I also read at my pole barn, at my brother's home in Florida, and at a rental resort on a weekend vacation.

- **Mood music can help.** I created soothing background noise to block out distractions. I used classical piano pieces on low volume. No lyrics to catch my attention. No guitar solos to get me emotionally fired up. No heavy beat to cover the steady beat of the words read off the page.

- **Mark it up!** Do you use highlighters or keep notes in your Bible? I do both. For this experiment, I went out and bought the latest edition of the NIV Bible. Imagine, a new Bible and I immediately started marking it up! I suggest you use whatever Bible translation you feel comfortable reading. A translation in modern English makes reading and understanding easier, but the old English of the King James Version works too. Make your Bible a working tool. Highlight chapter themes, important names and places, and, especially, every familiar and beloved passage in the Bible. I have given my children Bibles with my notes and highlights before. My 180 Bible is intended for my granddaughter on her confirmation day.

◯ **Find your pace.** Studying for 180 days is a long time. However, knowing this, I did not do my experiment for 180 days straight. Life got in the way. Two of my daughters each had a new baby. Grandkids got sick, then sick again . . . and then sick again. Guess what happened next? Grandpa got sick. I had to get real. I wanted to do my 180 days of personal spiritual growth and chose to accomplish that by doing three days a week. Sundays were days off for worship. And every other day of my week (or three days in a row some weeks) was a 180 day. This proved doable for me. What if you chose another timetable for your study? One week a month for 25 months. Every other week for a year. Thirty days, with a month off, then back for thirty days until you finish. Find what works for you. I am practical in my thinking. If you are disciplined and able to do an exercise program that promises a gorgeous body in 90 days, then go 180 days straight for your 180. I pray you find that you will feel great and have lean, strong, spiritual "muscles"! Make spiritual growth a priority for a lifetime. Pick a set time and stick with it. Make your spiritual turnaround (your 180) a thoughtful, regular practice.

Still with me? Would you like to start? Pen in hand and journal open, turn your Bible to the beginning. Remember, we read not only for information (the four "W's") but also for meditation (remember the questions on page 7). I'll get you started.

DAY 1

On my day 1, my daughter was four days overdue to have her third child. I was anxious for her. I had never felt this kind of concern when my wife and I were having children together. On this first day of my experiment, I was also remembering an anniversary: my oldest sister died and went to heaven ten years ago. I remembered complications, emergency room procedures, and a telephone call I couldn't believe was true. Lord, I believe. Help my unbelief! I want to trust you in everything!

What's happening in your life? Why did you start your 180 today?

Pray: Lord, thank you for faith. I am grateful to trust in you. I ask you, please, send your Holy Spirit into my heart, and wherever trust is lacking, fill in the gaps and give me the ability to rely on you no matter what happens this day. I ask this, trusting in Jesus. Amen.

Read: Genesis 1:1–2:2

FROM MY JOURNAL

- I noticed that in Genesis 1:1-2, "God" is mentioned as the Creator, but "the Spirit of God" was also present on the first day. Look at the table of contents in the front of your Bible. Find the page number for John and then turn to John 1:1-14. "The Word" is another name for Jesus (John 1:14). From the beginning, God identifies himself as the triune God—Father, Son, and Holy Spirit.
- Does Genesis chapter 1 try to convince me that God exists or that I must believe what is recorded here? The Bible never tries to prove that God exists. It simply tells me to trust in what that real and true God has said and done.

- Notice that power, real power, surrounded every creative word spoken by the Lord. Do you trust that God's power fills the pages of your Bible?

Review Romans 10:17. Why can you be confident of success in your 180?

JOURNAL YOUR THOUGHTS

Who: _____

What: _____

When: _____

Where: _____

What does this reading teach me about God? _____

_____

What does this reading teach me about sin? _____

_____

What does this reading teach me about God's love and forgiveness in Christ Jesus? _____

_____

How does this reading help me with trusting God more? _____

_____

Did you get a feel for how this works? I shared my own prayer with you for day 1. In the days ahead I encourage you to write, or simply pray, a prayer of your own as you begin. I invite you to continue for six more days.

DAY 2

Pray (*write your own*): _____

_____

Read: Genesis 2:4-25; 3:1-24

FROM MY JOURNAL

- Genesis 2:4-14 is an instant replay of Genesis chapter 1. We get to look more closely at creation and the first moments of life for the first people. Suddenly—BOOM!—there we are at the garden home of God's perfect people. One tree in the middle of Eden gave life. Perfect people were meant to live forever! Another tree near the same location granted knowledge of good and evil. On the one hand, to refuse to eat of this second tree was good, demonstrating love, trust, and obedience to God. But on the other hand, to eat of this tree was evil, evidence of a lack of love, trust, and obedience to God.

- In Genesis chapter 3, you and I meet the devil for the first time. He is real. He is a fallen angel. He uses camouflage. He is a liar and murderer. He is the enemy of faith (read 1 John 3:8; Revelation 12:9; John 8:44; and 1 Peter 5:8). As I read this section of Genesis, I remembered doing a door-to-door spiritual survey while working out west. After surveying thousands of households, I found that more people trusted that there was a devil than those who trusted in a loving God! Do you believe it?

- The world's first people contaminated creation with sin when they failed to love and trust God and disobeyed their Creator. Watch the reactions of our first parents and notice how this affected their faith relationship with God. Genesis 3:15 is the first promise of the Savior. God would rescue his children by overcoming and destroying the devil. The promise of the Savior is as old as history and just as important then as it is now. God never reneges on his promises! What does faith do with that?

JOURNAL YOUR THOUGHTS

(Feel free to use the eight questions that were outlined on day 1. You can find them on page 11.) **Keep going!**

_____
_____
_____
_____
_____
_____
_____
_____
_____
_____
_____
_____

DAY 3

Pray (*write your own*): _____
_____

Read: Genesis 4–5

FROM MY JOURNAL

- Sin passes from fallen parents to their children. I am infected with this disease of the soul and so are you. Our sin within fights faith. Does it always feel that way?

- Cain was the world's first unbeliever. The main difference between Cain's sacrifice and Abel's sacrifice is that Abel offered his sacrifice out of faith in God, while Cain did not. God accepted Abel's offering because of faith (read Hebrews 11:4).
- Yes, people lived longer in the early days of history. There are many possible reasons for this, but the greatest reason was God's will. God wanted the earth populated. This age thing presents a challenge to our faith. Does trusting more in the Lord mean trusting scientific theory less?

JOURNAL YOUR THOUGHTS

(Feel free to use the eight questions that were outlined on day 1. You can find them on page 11.) **Keep going!**

DAY 4

Pray (*write your own*): _____

_____

Read: Genesis 6

FROM MY JOURNAL

- The world went rogue leading up to the time of the flood, all except for Noah and his family. Is this a concern today and a possible threat to faith?
- I notice God's feelings toward sinful rebellion listed here. Is this still the way he feels about sin? My sin?
- Noah "found favor" with God (Genesis 6:8). God gave Noah grace just as he has given grace to you and me. Notice that by ordering a rescue barge, God was providing the way for the promise of the Savior to be preserved. The bloodline of Jesus would be on that ark. God was constantly aware of his promise to save us.
- Is our trust constantly/occasionally/rarely aware of God's saving love? Reflect on how clear and constant God's promises are, like those described in the simple words of the hymn "Jesus Loves Me." How does it affect our trust knowing that God is constantly aware of his promises to us?

JOURNAL YOUR THOUGHTS

(Feel free to use the eight questions that were outlined on day 1. You can find them on page 11.) **Keep going!**

_____

_____

_____

_____

_____

_____

_____

_____

_____

_____

_____

_____

_____

DAY 5

Pray (*write your own*): _____

_____

Read: Genesis 7

FROM MY JOURNAL

- God does not leave sin unpunished. Sin destroys my relationship with him. It certainly did for those destroyed by the flood. Recognizing this, I take my own sin very seriously. I confess it to God and look to him in faith for a rescue. In my 180, I stopped here to confess my sins, all my sins, every sin that ever angered my God. I didn't ask God to give me what I deserve. I asked for mercy. Does it matter if you trust God for justice (giving what a sin deserves) or mercy (giving the opposite of what a sin deserves)? Let me put it another way. When it comes to trusting God more, what do you wrestle with most: believing that God can and will bring justice to you (or others), believing that God can and will be merciful to you (or others), or believing that God can and will be both absolutely just and absolutely merciful at the same time? After picking one of these, ask yourself why. In what area is my trust in God the strongest? In what area could my trust in God use the most growth? Journal about it.

- Noah and his family trusted God for mercy. God used an ark to save Noah. God used a cross to save us. I am thankful and fascinated by a loving God who used destruction to raise believers above the destruction! Agree or disagree: Through the flood God demonstrates both his justice and his mercy. Agree or disagree: On the cross God demonstrates both his justice and his mercy. I'd love to hear your answers.
- The earth was covered by floodwaters. Think about this account and then think back to the account of creation. Do popular science and beliefs ever challenge faith in what God says in the Bible? Will I trustingly listen to God no matter what anyone else might say?

JOURNAL YOUR THOUGHTS

(Feel free to use the eight questions that were outlined on day 1. You can find them on page 11.) **Keep going!**

DAY 6

Pray (*write your own*): _____

_____

Read: Genesis 8

FROM MY JOURNAL

- The rain stopped and slowly the floodwaters diminished. Imagine being in the ark for more than a year and then leaving it to see the world changed after a devastating flood. What would be your first concerns after leaving the ark? What are most of our concerns even without catastrophe?

- Noah worshiped God with sacrifices. His trust in the Lord was shining like the sun! How do you see that happening as one of every seven clean animals was burnt up and given back to God? I asked myself, "Would my faith be strong enough for me to do the same with one-seventh of what is in my cupboard? my freezer? my bank account?"

- God's promise to never again destroy the whole earth with a flood is still in effect today. Take time to mull over Genesis 8:22 and, if the season is right, take a walk outside. What does this knowledge do to our worries? I know what it did to mine!

JOURNAL YOUR THOUGHTS

(Feel free to use the eight questions that were outlined on day 1. You can find them on page 11.) **Keep going!**

_____

_____

_____

_____

_____

DAY 7

Pray (*write your own*): _____
_____

Read: Genesis 9

FROM MY JOURNAL

- God blessed the eight believers who came off the ark, and they witnessed a rainbow as a sign of continued blessing. Remember this when you see your next rainbow! I look for rainbows after every storm. I saw a beauty the other day!
- Noah is not a perfect man. Believers are not perfect people. Why does the Bible remind me of this?
- Do you see the paradox in the flood account? God hates sin and must punish it. Yet, God loves you, dear believer, and will do anything to save you from this punishment. Identify for yourself how God managed this seeming conflict and worked out our forgiveness.

JOURNAL YOUR THOUGHTS

(Feel free to use the eight questions that were outlined on day 1. You can find them on page 11.) **Keep going!**

_____

_____

_____

_____

_____

_____

_____

_____

_____

_____

_____

_____

Seven days down . . . only 173 to go! I pray you see a blessing already. Do you know what it looks like when you trust God more? Keep going!

Our Journey's Destination

God blessed my daughter, after being overdue for a week, with the successful delivery of a baby boy. God is so good! My thankfulness filled my journal. I trusted him as life was going great! I even worked on my tan for a week in Florida. I was open to the Lord directing my 180. I was conscious of faith as I watched what and whom God sent into my life. I listened with my heart and took in all that was around me even as I continued to pray, study, and journal. I walked through my days trusting the Lord.

That being said, I was still not exactly sure what I was looking for with "more trust." If you are on the hunt for something, it helps to know the identity of your target. You will hunt in very different places and use different methods depending on whether you are bargain-hunting for antiques, carefully searching for filed documents, or looking through a scope for a 30-point buck. You know the best place to look when you are certain of what you are looking for. So what does our target—increased trust . . . BIG trust . . . strong/Stronger/STRONGEST TRUST—look like? I trusted that I would know it when I saw it!

I sat at the kitchen table just thinking. I know John 3:16. I know even the smallest trust in Jesus as the Savior can save. "A bruised reed he will not break, and a smoldering wick he will not snuff out" (Isaiah 42:3). More trust? Trusting God more? Oh, how I've failed in situations when I haven't trusted or when my faith has faced a wall of opposition! Did

Jesus ever find and define "great faith" or "super trust"? I took out my concordance. Some Bibles have this included in the back of the book. Mine happens to be a separate book. It lists every word used in the Bible and lists every time that same word is used in a passage. I looked up *faith* and there it was! Jesus described individual faith as great only twice in his three-year ministry. I looked up the references. Sadly, this wasn't said about the 12 disciples. Great trust was not theirs . . . yet. They were like us, followers of Jesus with a lot of growing to do!

It surprised me that in both cases, the owners of praiseworthy trust were not even Jewish. The nation of Israel was privileged. God gave the people of Israel his blessing. He spoke to them through his Word. The Savior of the world shared their ancestry. Yet not one of Jesus' race or family was recognized in the New Testament for a great faith. Rather, it was a Roman centurion (Matthew 8:5-13; Luke 7:1-10) and a Canaanite woman (Matthew 15:21-28) who were recognized for their great faith.

I'll tell you what I remembered. A centurion was a military officer, typically with 80 to 100 men under his command. This centurion made friends with his Jewish neighbors. He built them a house of worship. He cared deeply even for those who were his servants. The centurion's servant was very ill: paralysis and extreme pain (Matthew 8:6) and on the verge of death (Luke 7:2). Elders from the city of Capernaum pleaded with Jesus to help this Roman officer. The centurion himself learned of Jesus and asked him to rescue his beloved employee. But when Jesus offered to come to his house to perform this miracle, the centurion declined the offer. He trusted that Jesus could heal long-distance! Just as the centurion commanded men to carry out orders and they did it, Jesus could say the word and disease would disappear and health would return. Say the word, Jesus! Do I have confidence it only takes a word from Jesus to answer my prayers? That's trusting!

Celebrate with me! Jesus did say the word. The healing happened. And Jesus appreciated something unique. Christ said, "I tell you, I have not found such great faith even in Israel" (Luke 7:9). Do we have trust that is so praiseworthy? I don't yet . . . but I'd like to!

Now the other "great faith" quotation. It involves a Canaanite woman. Her homeland was renowned for its unbelief. Throughout Old Testament history, Canaanites were the sworn enemies of God's people. They were famous for idol worship and for leading God's children away from the Lord to a life of excess and promiscuity. There's the family tree for this troubled lady!

Her trouble? Her daughter was demon-possessed. Somehow, she had heard of Jesus and his power to help. Her faith in Jesus made her grab this hope with both hands. She shared with Jesus that her daughter was suffering terribly. I guarantee you, more than love for a child had this mother upset. When the devil would send a demon into a person's life, bizarre things would happen: pain, seizures, crippling illness, suicidal tendencies, supernatural strength and knowledge, and outbursts of physical abuse against the possessed and others (all symptoms recorded in the New Testament). The Bible paints a terrifying picture of this malady. Imagine a mother coming home to any or all of this. She needed power to free her child from this hellish grip! She needed heaven's help! She needed Jesus!

I was surprised that our Lord seemed less than caring about this woman's plight. Or was he? He seems to play the prejudice card as his reason to refuse her. If I'm not mistaken, Jesus suggested this mother was a dog compared to the children of God.

But her trust would not be stymied. Her faith held tightly to Jesus even though he seemed to refuse her. She focused on a suffering child, her desperate circumstances, and what she believed to be her Savior's love and power. Trust would not let go. The words just blurted out of her mouth: "Even the dogs eat the crumbs that fall from their master's table" (Matthew 15:27). In other words, "I won't even argue with you, Lord. I'm a dog in comparison to your family. I don't deserve even a slice of bread for a meager meal. But I'm looking to my master for crumbs. I'm happy to have crumbs. Just crumbs, Jesus!" I tear up just thinking about her confidence and confession.

All along, Jesus was testing what he already saw in that woman's heart. Jesus told her, "Woman, you have great faith! Your request is granted"

(Matthew 15:28). Jesus sent the demon out of the girl, where it didn't belong, and sent a child back into her mother's arms where she belonged. Do you have any doubt that the mother and daughter both rested in Jesus' arms from that day on? Do you begin to see what more trust looks like?

After two replaced knees, I don't kneel anymore. But in my soul, I was on my "prayer bones" asking:

> Dearest Lord, that's what I want, and I want this for all who join me in this pursuit. Cause our trust to increase. Draw it from me. Test it and temper it until it is strong! This is not just another shiny thing I want to possess. This is not for bragging rights to feed my overinflated ego. To trust completely so that my heart is your heart and my hope belongs to you—this is what I ask. Please allow my life to rest only on you! Amen.

I prayed it that day . . . after God showed me two examples of trusting him more.

Help me identify characteristics of increased faith that trusts God more because of the working of his grace:

1. More trust is not like supersized fries that somehow make me bigger or greater. Look at the centurion and the Canaanite woman. They didn't make their own faith great and then show it off for Jesus to see. God made their faith great. Had they seen firsthand any of the miracles that Jesus performed? Had they heard him preach? Maybe they had only heard about Jesus from others, but regardless of how they learned of him, the words and actions of Jesus hit home. God is generous. God is merciful. God can and will help. God used the message of Jesus to create faith in their hearts and then made that faith soar to great new heights. Jesus can help. More than that, Jesus is willing to help. Jesus is greater than the problems and challenges that I face. He can do anything, and he does! Great faith comes from a great God! Reflect on

that. How great is your God? Has he shown that he can do anything that is right and serves his purpose for you? Absolutely. Can he overcome any predicament, obstacle, or enemy to faith? The Bible proves it. He can overcome hell itself and even tell demons to stand down and they obey him. So what problem or challenge are you facing that led you to pick up this study? Who or what will cause your faith to become great?

2. Greater trust means absolute confidence in God's Word. If Jesus says it, it will happen. The power of heaven itself backs Christ's promises. Ask the centurion or his servant and you would get the reply, "If Jesus says it, he does it, and that's that for me! Hoo-ah!" Ask the Canaanite mother or her daughter and each would say, "If Jesus appears to be hesitating, forget appearances! He loves you! Humbly keep believing and keep on asking! Trust him!" What discourages your trust?

3. Great trust expects great blessings from Jesus. Trust isn't feeble. The Bible writer James said that it is not wise to ask our generous God for something and then doubt you will receive it (James 1:5-8). The Holy Spirit, on the other hand, creates and strengthens trust so we can confidently believe that God will answer all our prayers for Jesus' sake. Trust says, "I talked to Jesus' Father about it. The One who is so generous to me in Christ will take care of everything!" Is this the thing that is dragging down my trust? Is God taking care of . . . everything?

Increasing our trust may never put us among the elite of believers. But it doesn't have to. Wouldn't you love for Jesus to look into your heart and say, "I haven't seen such trusting faith in all of your hometown, your state, or even your country"? But really, is that all we are after? To simply be complimented by Jesus for our great faith? No! When others are discouraged in their faith, I ask him for a faith that shows greater courage and demonstrates it by trust. I desire the gift of a trust that expects real solutions and answers to my troubles because God promises that his love for me is that great! I want to go to bed each night certain that the Lord loves me and that everything is going to be alright! Add that to my list of things to continue praying for.

I'm ready to let God inspire such a trust, feed it with his promises, and watch it grow! Are you with me? Get your journal, say your prayer, open your Bible, and let's get answers to some "W's."

TIPS ALONG THE WAY

○ **Review your steps.** You may need to review the process of your 180 in chapter 2. Do it. Turn on some background music, get comfortable, and get ready to do some reading. Don't forget the highlighter! Mark every name, place, or passage that seems important to you.

○ **Everyone learns differently.** If reading is difficult for you, there are audio Bible CDs, online services, or apps available. Even better, ask someone else to join with you and read for your 180. If someone else is reading aloud, I still suggest following along in your Bible. Following verse by verse helps to hold your attention as eyes, ears, and hands all work together on your meditation.

○ **Ready to go on your own?** Format your journal in a way that works for you. But try to follow the same outline (your "W's" and the additional questions) that we used the first seven days. I won't add them anymore, but you can write them into your journal. They're important for each day's digging. Each reading will still have study points for you to think about along the way.

Now, please join me in studying an Old Testament believer you know as Abram or Abraham. He was an amazing man of God and a brother in faith. Some call him the father of believers.

DAY 8

Pray

Read: Genesis 12

FROM MY JOURNAL

- I skimmed through Genesis chapters 10 and 11. Each generation of descendants proves God's faithfulness to his post-flood promises. He can be trusted! Now, what did Abram's trust in the Lord move him to leave? How old was he at the time? Starting over for what?

- As I read this, I wonder, "What would more trust give you strength to do and to let go of? I am a retired American Christian on Social Security and Medicare with a small pension and very attached to my extended family. My doctors, dentist, and pharmacy are all a cell phone call and a short drive away. My mechanic, grocer, and favorite restaurant are all in my backyard. What if God asked me to start over in China?" Look at Abram's example. What if God is challenging you to keep trusting while your life is drastically changing? How would you approach it?

- Egypt was the breadbasket of the ancient world. If there was a famine, folks migrated to the land of the Nile. After brilliant faith took Abram to Palestine, that same faith stumbled down in Egypt. Abram exposed Sarai (later known as Sarah) to a sexually compromising moment because he feared for his own neck! Ouch! Remember, the Bible doesn't shy away from sharing believers' flaws. Note: Right beside trust live fear, doubt, and worry. They are found even in the lives of the most trusting believers. And yet, great trust is inspired by the great, loving, forgiving God.

- Do you have memories of a stumbling faith? Do a little experiment with me. Fill a glass half full of water. I used my half-full coffee cup. Tip the glass back and forth, from one side to the other. Watch what the water does on either side of the glass as you rock it back and forth. Do you notice a wave beginning to form in your cup? High points are soon followed by low points. The same can be true in our life of faith. Next time I have a shining moment of great trust, I must be on my guard. If I am not careful when my trust is riding high, I could find myself drifting from highs to lows in my life of faith. On the other hand, when I catch myself at a low point in my faith, I turn once again to God's promises to love me, forgive me, and bless me. God's next blessing, which I may not be able to see now, may suddenly appear and make my trust swell even higher.

JOURNAL YOUR THOUGHTS

DAY 9

Pray

Read: Genesis 13–14

FROM MY JOURNAL

- People who trust in the Lord still have trouble in the workplace, even when (or maybe because) their coworkers are relatives. Faith is practical! I see it in action in the life of Abram. Look how Abram solves problems with Lot. Abram's trust in God made him a good manager of business and family. God promised Abram *all* the land.
- Why do you think God repeated his promise to Abram? Why can my faith afford to be generous? Has trust in God given me a generous nature?
- Lot's choices resulted in great danger to his family and himself. Trusting God, Abram and an outnumbered force attacked an enemy army. I learn plenty right here about trust in action. When facing a battle in life, I shouldn't determine my course of action based on the size of the opposition. Remember what I shared on day 8? "Great faith comes from a _____!" What battles are you fighting? And are you equal to the odds? Write about it in your journal.

JOURNAL YOUR THOUGHTS

DAY 10

Pray

Read: Genesis 15–17

FROM MY JOURNAL

- Increased trust does not mean immediate prosperity or every prayer answered just as I want it. Faith remains faith: believing something will be, even though there is no tangible proof. Abram wanted children. God gave him promises that filled the skies! If faith wavers, God's promises prove to be "the breakfast of champions." At this point, I took time to remember Romans 10:17. Chew on God's promises!

- Faith offers us a credit plan. Review Genesis 15:6. God credits us with righteousness through faith. We don't have righteousness, a right standing with God, on our own, so God advances one to you and me. Check out Galatians 3:6-9,13-14. Why do we desperately need Jesus in order to have credit with heaven?

- In Genesis chapter 17, the Lord introduced himself as God Almighty, *El Shaddai* in Hebrew. God is powerful and can do anything. Consider that Abram was 99 years old and Sarai was 89. Consider the mess Sarai made with Hagar and now another promise that God would greatly increase Abram's numbers. God better be almighty. What's he working with for this reproductive miracle? I looked at my wrinkles and shook my head!

- Sarai tried to fulfill a promise only God can accomplish. How did that work out? Have you ever trusted God and asked him to do something for you, only to rip it out of his hands so that you can supposedly do it better? I have been there. Do you run after quick fixes? How's that working?

JOURNAL YOUR THOUGHTS

DAY 11

Pray

Read: Genesis 18–19

FROM MY JOURNAL

- God and two angels take on the appearance of normal human visitors. Their sudden appearance and their knowledge of Sarah proved that they were more than mere men. Notice that they used her newly changed name and later knew exactly what she had done! God and angels came to visit and lunch with Abraham like they were old friends! Do I trust that God is my friend? that he likes being with me? that he sends angels to protect my home or business?

- Old age made Sarah laugh in unbelief at the promise of a son. Medical science was against her prospects of motherhood. She laughed! God knew immediately! God knows everything: our circumstances, our medical concerns, and our spiritual lacks and wants. This frightens me a little but also comforts me. Despite what God saw in Sarah, his promise was unwavering and as good as fulfilled! Do I laugh in disbelief at promises that call for trust and thanksgiving?

- God dealt his judgment against the cities of Sodom and Gomorrah. Their wickedness, immorality, and violence screamed for divine justice. I wonder if the United States is any better off in God's sight. I ask, "Am I any better?" Sins may vary, but every sin is equally damning. All those sins put Jesus on the cross . . . yet Jesus went willingly to the cross!

- Review John 3:16 and 1 John 1:5-10. I took time to confess my sins, those that still bother me and those I have forgotten. I deserve fire and brimstone; I do! As I trust more and more, I feel the need for Jesus more and more. My 180 is an oasis where I crawl, dying of thirst, and Jesus loves me and gives me the living water of forgiveness. He gives himself for me!

- Don't pass by these chapters and fail to see God's holy outrage with our sin. Then read Abraham's prayer for mercy again. In Christ, God showed mercy to "50 . . . 45 . . . 40 . . . 30 . . . 20 . . . 10" and, in reality, to 1—me! Oh, wait. He showed mercy to 2—me and you! Do I pray for mercy for people caught in sin? God has mercy to spare! Do I trust that God hears and answers this prayer? Look, even Lot and his daughters needed a prayer for mercy.

JOURNAL YOUR THOUGHTS

DAY 12

Pray

Read: Genesis 20–21

FROM MY JOURNAL

- God must intervene yet again because Abraham, who has had visits from God himself and has promises to bless the ages, was afraid. I thought Abraham's faith was well-fed. Two things popped into my mind.

    1. Watch out for sins of weakness. I know I have sin that appeals to my lack of spiritual strength or preys on me because I'm weak. "Lord, intervene for me!" You promise to make me equal to the task of fighting temptation (1 Corinthians 10:12-13).

    2. God's work to increase my trust is never done in this life, even if I have the same level of faith as Abraham. I need to stay in God's promises all my life so that he can nourish and strengthen my faith.

- The birth of Isaac was a high point for Abraham and Sarah. God kept his promise, and the proof of his faithfulness rested at Sarah's breast. Yet the new child also gave birth to new resentment and abuse from Hagar and Ishmael. Will more trust in the Lord immediately (or ever) erase all family strife?

- Check Genesis 21:12-13. Would trust relieve stress? Would that work in my home?
- Strife with neighbors is also an ongoing problem. Even with increased trust in the Lord, we are sinners and so are the neighbors. Watch Abraham. Trust in the Lord made him speak to Abimelek in a direct manner. Trusting God's power, who do I need to talk to more directly about a problem?

JOURNAL YOUR THOUGHTS

DAY 13

Pray

Read: Genesis 22

FROM MY JOURNAL

- Even the greatest trust needs to be tested. Testing proves strengths and uncovers weaknesses. God is not cruel when he puts me to the test. He shows me where faith still needs to grow. Abraham passed the test with flying colors! Read Hebrews 11:17-19. What did Abraham trust to happen even as he lifted the knife?
- Note: In a unique act of love, the heavenly Father gave his Son to save us. And Jesus willingly offered himself on the cross to win forgiveness and heaven for all. The Bible also tells of false religions and heathen sacrifices of children. Our God never asks us to offer human sacrifice.
- Read 1 Peter 1:17-19. God bought us back from a life of sin and death "with the precious blood of Christ, a lamb without blemish or defect." In place of Isaac's life, God provided a substitute that was sacrificed. I imagine myself on the altar. A sharp knife is raised and ready to strike its mark! But the blade never touches me. It strikes another: the substitute!

JOURNAL YOUR THOUGHTS

DAY 14

Pray

Read: Genesis 23:1–25:11

FROM MY JOURNAL

- Isaac needed a wife for the lineage of Abraham and, ultimately, the bloodline of Christ to continue. However, not just any wife would do. Abraham's faith in the promise led him to great lengths to arrange for a marriage with a God-fearing woman. My faith relationship with the Lord was a major factor in my dating, courtship, and marriage. How important do you consider a believing spouse? During my 180, I stopped to thank God for my believing wife and the years of encouragement she has given to my faith.

- After Sarah died, Abraham remarried. He was blessed with more family, and he cared for them as he prepared for his own death. Isaac received the inheritance, but all of Abraham's children experienced the blessing of a believing parent. I asked, "How will my children and grandchildren be blessed by me when I go to heaven?" The answer to that question is being lived today! How will your family remember that your life was one of trust in the Lord?

JOURNAL YOUR THOUGHTS

Fourteen days down . . . only 166 to go! God bless faith!

Family: Looking Back at the Road Already Traveled

Note: *This chapter contains content dealing with physical abuse.*

Retirement and a 180 give you time to think. Where have you been in the walk of faith? You remember your childhood, your home of origin, your relationship with siblings and parents. So watch out now! We are going into an area where trust goes home—that is, back to our roots, when we first learned about what it means to trust in God and what it means to trust other people—where trust must navigate feelings and emotions, and where trust is tested and proven. What are your memories of growing up? I pray they were all hugs and kisses, seasoned with sugar cookies. Sometimes family life is like that, or at least it can give that impression. But appearances to outsiders often vaporize when piercing eyes search for facts and truth.

I believe that every family is dysfunctional to some degree, including mine. Sin makes every relationship toxic. Our homes are not always havens of love and support. Family members, due to sin and fatigue and weakness, fail one another and fail a God who expects us to be a blessing to one another in our family units.

I was the second child and oldest son in a family of four children. I have two sisters and one brother. My mother was a Christian and was raised in a Christian home. My father was the son of Transylvanian immigrants and was brought up in a home where faith was cultural, two spoken languages was practical, and attitudes were very old country. After meeting my mother, my father learned of Jesus. After he was instructed, he was baptized and confirmed on the same day.

My parents were "every Sunday" worshipers. Although we lived only two blocks from church, we ended up marching into services during the singing of the last verse of the first hymn. And we had to sit right up front, in the second pew, beneath the pulpit. (The first pew was unofficially reserved for another family that trailed in behind us at the "Amen!") As kids, we were in Sunday school, vacation Bible school, and Lutheran elementary school. In the 1950s and 1960s, we looked and lived like suburban Americans.

Influenced by this week's Bible readings, my 180 brought back bad memories. I feel bad laying this on you, yet this is one of the reasons I needed to trust God more in my youth. My father was a "good-time guy" to his friends but an angry man at home. He never hit my mother, and I don't remember him ever laying a hand on my sisters. He taught me, "Boys don't hit girls! Never!" However, my father's example taught me, "Boys do verbally abuse and intimidate girls." The ladies in my home felt the sting of cursing and insults. I'm a grown man, yet as I sat recalling my childhood, I sat at the table weeping. I remember loud tirades and chaos as loved ones scattered to get out of Daddy's way.

My earthly father was a perfectionist but not a doer. Perfectionism, and what may have been a bipolar disorder, kept him jumping from job to job until later in life when he became a US postal worker. He saw himself as an ambassador, representing the government by serving neighborhood citizens. He wasn't nearly as diplomatic with his sons. Brutal in criticism, he was impossible to please. Without instruction or demonstration, he'd order us to manicure the yard, paint the garage, and maintain outdoor equipment. Can you see it? It was a disaster waiting to happen. How much does a nine-year-old know about internal combustion engines? I didn't know they needed oil. I only knew that gas made them run. With school grades, sports participation, and the big one, behavior, he demanded perfection or commanded an angry "You can't do anything right. How could any child of mine be such a loser?"

My little brother was berated and bullied. But after witnessing how my father made me a "man," my mother shielded him from most of the physical abuse. I was not protected. I regularly went to school decorated with welts and bruises. I could take a punch better than any kid my age. I learned to let Dad go first down the stairs or risk being literally kicked down a flight of steps and landing in a heap at the bottom. "Stop crying or I'll give you something to cry about! If people ask you what happened, tell them you tripped." After my father's funeral, my sister awarded me my dad's razor strap. It was a tool for polishing and straightening old-fashioned razors. I knew its bite very well. She said, "This should be yours." I walked outside in front of crying relatives and burned it in a fire. My family cried for me.

Did I ever promise that your 180 would be pain free? Reflect. Remember. Cry if you must. Please journal. Oh, and look to God's Word for help and hope! When you don't understand your life or its trouble, God's Word beckons you to trust even more!

Some say that your relationship with your earthly father determines your image of the heavenly Father. That was not true for me, and I pray that unless you had a wonderful relationship with a firm but loving dad, it is not true for you. Something quite different happened to me. I had a perfect Father who built me up and protected me when life was hell-bent on breaking me down. He is Jesus' Father too. His address is H-E-A-V-E-N. I would run to him with my pain and look to him for perfect love . . . and he always gave it! He sent his Son, Jesus, to walk me through each situation and remind me to forgive my angry parent.

Jesus would remind me that my earthly dad was a struggling Christian who needed time to grow . . . that I needed to obey, respect, and love my biological father because it was my heavenly Father's will for me. Jesus taught me to control my own anger issues and fight to protect those who couldn't protect themselves. Good news for my own children, grandchildren, and . . . me! My perfect, loving Father always keeps his promise: "We know that in all things God works for the good of those who love him, who have been called according to his purpose" (Romans 8:28). Making a bad situation good is God's specialty!

My dad struggled with his anger all his life. One minute, he could turn on the charm and be delightful, and the next moment, he was a raging abuser. But the heavenly Father arranged a revelation for my dad before his death. He was summoned for jury duty. It happened to be a child abuse case, with a written history of physical violence and pictures to prove it. My dad actually said this: "In my day, that would be nothing. Why, I did worse than that to my . . ." He choked on the last word. At the end of the trial, he agreed with his fellow jurors and found the man guilty as charged. However, God was at work and convicted my father too.

At breakfast, during one of my visits to care for him and my mom, he said, "I suppose you think I abused you too." I said, "Yes, you did. And if it happened today, they would arrest you, jail you, and send your children to someone else for care." He and my mother melted into a puddle of tears. He begged me to forgive him. I told him, "I already have a thousand times and also every time I remember and feel my own rage that this ever happened." Our heavenly Father asks us to forgive for the sake of Jesus' love and sacrifice. Forgiveness is the best gift I have ever received or have ever given my dad. The Spirit moved it. The Son applauded it. My Father in heaven smiled his approval.

TIPS ALONG THE WAY

○ **God's Word never looks the other way.** This week's readings may be rough for you. The Bible records history without fluff or excuse. Abraham's children sinned against one another. God did not condone their favoritism, lies, or abuse. However, the scriptural text does not record God's immediate admonition or condemnation of their behavior. God could have responded immediately with judgment and justice. Instead, he responded with patience and grace.

○ **Remember that every person struggles with sin.** We tend to rank sins as greater or smaller, especially if we are trying to explain away our own offenses. All sins nailed Jesus to the cross. Your journal is your personal reflection on old memories. Remember, others may not know how much their sins hurt us. They don't see the negative effect their actions have had on our lives. When is it the right time to confront them and open that conversation? Is there a right time to tell all? I seriously struggled with what was called family business: dark secrets to be hidden. I also wrestled with what must remain quiet to protect the innocent. You were spared details.

○ **Never hesitate to reach out for help.** I have been a counselor to victims of physical and sexual abuse by family members. The hurt and humiliation of such sin may require professional help. Your 180 may need to include an appointment with your pastor, with social services, with the police, or with a trained victim and grief counselor.

○ **Forgiveness is possible.** Try to remember all or any good that came from your home of origin. I learned to fish and hunt from my dad, to play cards, and to keep a cool head in an emergency. Know it is possible to love someone deeply while hating their sin and abuse. Learn from the heavenly Father. He hates sin completely and loves us unconditionally at the same time!

- **Ask God to help you love others as much as he loves you.** Your 180 may lead you to the conclusion that it is time to forgive Mom, Dad, sisters, brothers, extended family, or others. Spend some time with Jesus at the cross. Our sins put him there, yet he spent his dying breath praying, "Father, forgive them, for they do not know what they are doing" (Luke 23:34). Couldn't this be said of our relations too? "They didn't get it . . . they didn't realize . . . they were clueless"—just like me sometimes! Forgive for Jesus' sake, because of what Jesus did for you! You will be doing yourself a favor. Personal resentment only eats holes in your heart. Trust me, I know. Trust your Lord. Our Father knows best! Forgive, and when bitter thoughts resurface, forgive again!

- **Trust in God's grace and forgiveness for you.** What if you are the one who has made family life miserable? Don't avoid spending some time with Jesus at his cross. Instead, put your sins there and leave them with the One who takes them so completely away that God sees them no more. Walk away forgiven and go to the people you hurt and ask their forgiveness too. Moved by Jesus' love, ask the hurting how you can make things better.

Pick up your Bible and open the book of Genesis. Pray. Read. Journal. **Let's get started!**

DAY 15

Pray

Read: Genesis 25:12-34; 26–28

FROM MY JOURNAL

- Extended families fight. Read Genesis 25:18 while remembering that Arab nations and Israel are shirttail relatives! The immediate family wrestles for control and causes conflict. This time look no further than Jacob and Esau: favoritism, deceit, lies, manipulation, and hatred. They are as old as the history of God's children. Don't excuse bad behavior. Expose it to the light of Scripture. Repent of it and run to the cross!

- Do parents teach their children the sinful way around family and neighborhood politics? Abraham did. Isaac and Rebekah did. It appears the apple fell near the parental tree as Isaac deceived Abimelek. Our children and, for me, grandchildren are watching! Take note of what they learn.

JOURNAL YOUR THOUGHTS

DAY 16

Pray

Read: Genesis 29–31

FROM MY JOURNAL

- What goes around comes around. Jacob established a family in his temporary home. God allowed him to experience payback for his past deceit. I have experienced something like this myself. Is God being cruel in allowing consequences to happen to us after he has forgiven us? If not, I sometimes wonder, "What's he doing?" For just a moment, skip ahead to day 45 and read through the second

entry in "From My Journal." How can I trust God even more, even when he allows me to experience consequences?
- Competition can be fun at a sporting event. Watch out for competition in a marriage or in your extended family. I counted all the lies told in our readings. Try it; you'll be surprised. Family harmony cannot be built on fear and falsehood. As a child, I lived that. As I learn to trust God more, I would live above that!

JOURNAL YOUR THOUGHTS

DAY 17

Pray

Read: Genesis 32–34

FROM MY JOURNAL
- Tension filled Jacob on his trip home, and he planned for the worst. God, however, always works for the best! The Lord blessed Jacob even as he limped away from a sleepless night of wrestling. Jacob gleamed with sweat, ached after struggle, refused to let go of God, and left with a blessing. He was better for the experience! After you have seen the face of God, you are ready for anything! Are you afraid to go home? There was a time when I was. Have you wrestled it out with your God? Did you get a blessing?
- Esau got over the family intrigue and wholeheartedly forgave his brother. There comes a time in a family when we need to get over it and forgive. How would this homecoming have been different if Esau couldn't or wouldn't get over it? In Dinah's case, her brothers couldn't get over it. They wouldn't look for a happy ending after obvious sin. Do the sins of others justify our own terrible sins? Can I justify not letting go? How can trusting God more help me to let go?

JOURNAL YOUR THOUGHTS

DAY 18

Pray

Read: Genesis 35–38

FROM MY JOURNAL

- Sinful families need full assurance that a merciful God forgives them and restores them to his family. In Genesis 35:9-15, God came to Jacob, now called Israel, to repeat the promise given to Abraham. Sin did not disqualify Jacob from the promise that included a future Savior! Our God mercifully forgives and then looks ahead to a promised future, not behind to a history of wrongdoing. Trusting God more, do family members get the same break from me that Jacob received?
- They never stop: jealousy, hatred, anger, boasting, lies. Jacob's children were a wrecking crew to their family, causing tears and grief. Joseph was a victim. Sometimes we all are. Don't feel like the only one. Keep reading and learn how to grow out of a victim mentality.

JOURNAL YOUR THOUGHTS

DAY 19

Pray

Read: Genesis 39–41

FROM MY JOURNAL

- God is working even when (especially when) we can't see how. Joseph was knocked down again and again, but God, in his own time, raised him back up each time. What if I can't see this progression in my life right now? Trusting more leads to patience! Give the Lord time to work.

- Scripture does not promise that our dreams are prophetic, but if God wanted them to be, they would be. This reading is not a guide to interpreting night visions. God's power made this happen for Joseph, and God's plan made things turn out as they did. Jail time taught Joseph patience and humility. I never doubt that God was somehow shaping me through what I experienced as a kid. I think I could have done without it. But maybe not! God knows what he's doing!

JOURNAL YOUR THOUGHTS

DAY 20

Pray

Read: Genesis 42–45

FROM MY JOURNAL

- God has a plan. His plan brought Israel and his descendants to Egypt for an extended stay of four hundred years. God told Abraham it would be this way (Genesis 15:13-16). God's plan extends through generations of events! This helps me to believe that God has a plan no matter what life throws at me. Trusting God more, relax just a little. The plan is working!
- Joseph tested the sincerity of his brothers' repentance. They had grown beyond petty jealousy and hatred. Joseph's reveal was one for the books! News of Joseph reached and revived his dad. Good news does that. What is the value of celebrating the successes of our relationships rather than forever mourning the losses?

JOURNAL YOUR THOUGHTS

DAY 21

Pray

Read: Genesis 46–50

FROM MY JOURNAL

- Joseph used his power and influence to bless his Egyptian neighbors and growing family. Doesn't it amaze you that he outdistanced the trauma of his childhood? Trusting the Lord kept him from living in a rut. He and his children were blessed by this. I pray that my family is also a recipient of such blessing. I pray that your family is too.

- There is great fear in a dysfunctional family. Loved ones fear retaliation. What a great gift when God's love moves his trusting children to forgive rather than retaliate. That's my experience! I took time to consider Genesis 50:20-21. Joseph got it right!

JOURNAL YOUR THOUGHTS

Twenty-one days down . . . only 159 to go! Keep believing!

Friends: Helping Those Who Travel With Us

Note: *This chapter contains content dealing with sexual abuse, abortion, and suicidal thoughts.*

Last week was difficult. I pray it was a bittersweet effort to remember and journal about family. Know that as your trust continues to grow, you will have greater clarity and begin to better manage your feelings. Our thoughts will search for valuable keepsakes even in rags and rubble. That proved true for Joseph in Egypt and John in Wisconsin.

This week of prayer, study, meditation, and journaling will move us in a similar yet different direction. I want to introduce you to a friend who walks with us along the path to increased trust. She gave me her permission to share her story with you. I'll call her Heather for the purpose of sharing her story, and I have known her and her husband for years. They are on my short list of BFFs—best friends forever.

Whenever you think you are alone in a struggle of faith, know there are many people with equal or greater struggles. Sometimes their stories put life and faith into perspective. I met Heather at a low point in her life. I was a Christian friend to her, and over time, she told me her story.

She was a healthy, athletic, and happy girl who enjoyed her friends and playing basketball. Her family belonged to a Bible-teaching church in a small town where everyone knew one another's name . . . and business. She went to Sunday school and later to adult membership classes but confessed to me later in life, "Growing up you can't wait to become an adult member of your church so you don't have to go so much for instruction and worship. I believe many kids think like that, and, boy, are we wrong. Jesus needs to be in our lives all the time!"

The teen years proved a real struggle for Heather and her faith. When she was 16, an adult friend of the family manipulated a naïve and inexperienced young woman. She didn't understand the sexual side of life, and he kept grooming her response and pushing his agenda until what happened can only be described as molestation and rape. She told no one. She later told me, "If you know something is wrong, then please listen to your gut. Seek out an adult you can trust and tell them that things are not right." Heather harbored her fear and shame and looked for love and acceptance. Unfortunately, she found it in someone other than Jesus.

Another man, a boyfriend, came into the picture. Heather was in love, and he was in lust. He promised to support her. He promised marriage, so she considered them engaged. He left her in a predicament when she discovered she was unwed and quite pregnant. Some might say, "Put this behind you." Family said, "You are not ready for a child." No one was offering alternatives, while our American society was saying, "If life is inconvenient, get rid of it." Looking back, Heather said, "God says, 'Thou shalt not kill.' I knew that. I did kill a little person growing inside me. An abortion. How could I do that? It's the worst decision I ever made. . . . I took the easy way out . . . at first."

At first, Heather described herself as numb and relieved the pregnancy was over. She went on with her life, but she could not forget. She imagined the child was a little boy. She remembered what would have been his birthday. She gave the unborn child a name. And she got angry. Heather had always had a temper, but now the anger turned and fermented into rage.

Eventually, she married. A good-natured husband and a healthy baby daughter made her imagine that the past was behind her. Then came a second child, a baby boy. "They said he was healthy, but when he got a certain age," she recalled, "he would not follow you with his eyes as he was supposed to. The family doctor said we had reason for concern and sent us to an eye specialist. This turned into a dead end that led us to a major hospital and a thousand questions. The doctor in charge of our son's case finally said, 'The kindest diagnosis I can give you is cerebral palsy.'" Heather's life seemed to stop.

At six months old, the boy's seizures started. According to Heather, it was nothing for the baby to have 70 or more seizures in a single day. The family lived in the hospital. The local ministry dropped the ball, and Heather and her husband felt they were without faith support. Her anger began turning from the people who had wronged her to God, who had given her a special child. Heather imagined that her baby was God's punishment for her sins of the past, and as you might expect, anger turned into deep depression. She recalled, "Depression is something you can't control. Your feelings and emotions are everywhere. I learned to be two people: the one person that friends think they know and the one who is fighting to just get through a day." After several close relatives died, the devil used the opportunity to once again suggest an easy exit from pain. Anxiety pushed a struggling believer toward suicide.

Jesus kept that from happening. He still does. Loved ones continue to offer support to Heather, but her load in life is heavy. Attempts to help are often too little or too late. She has been hospitalized several times for emotional problems and given medications to ease suicidal thoughts.

Where's the high side of this story? God's grace has kept Heather in the Word and has kept her a part of the church. If you ask her, "Do you believe?" she will quickly confess faith in God, who has kept her from crashing her van into a bridge support. Heather prays every day, all day. She believes God is listening and can do miracles. She trusts that Jesus is with her and saves her. She fights self-destructive fantasies with thoughts of heaven. She tells the devil to go away and tells him she will do nothing to jeopardize her eternal life. She believes her son, now 29 years old, is a blessing from God and not a punishment. I asked her if she will be in heaven someday. She said, "Yes! Jesus loves me and died on the cross for the forgiveness of my sins, *all* my sins." She continually asks his grace to struggle through another day. Heather earnestly wants to trust God more. I still call and ask her how she is doing. She quotes Philippians 4:13: "I can do this through him [Jesus Christ] who gives me strength."

I asked her to start her own 180. She was ready—eager—and she said, "Yes!"

TIPS ALONG THE WAY

- **Consider sharing your story with a trusted friend.** My friend chose to share her story. After a lifetime of emotional and mental suffering, her hope and prayer are to serve God by helping you. Is Heather too broken for her 180? In any life we look at (yours and mine included), we can see a tangled web of sins. They are the sins done to us, the sins we have done to others, and life in a sin-fallen world. Ask God's help for a better tomorrow. Ask him to give you trusted friends for encouragement on the journey. Our Savior makes all of that possible. No one is too broken. We each may feel we are the most broken, the "worst of sinners" as Paul called himself in 1 Timothy 1:15-16. But Paul also reminds us that no one is too broken for Jesus!

- **Friends can help with trusting God more.** I have been thinking about how Heather helped me trust God more. She did. I was helping a friend but felt inadequate for the job. I'd pray for her. I'd comb the Scriptures looking for answers to her questions. She would ask me incredibly difficult questions. I'd share the Word and trust it was helping her even if I couldn't always see it. Could the doctor always see how the medication was working for her? My faith was challenged, but I thought, *Why do I expect to see an immediate response? Just keep trying to help!* I trusted the power of God's Word, not my words. That trust has grown.

- **Even through trouble, God strengthens trust in his love.** In the biblical story of Moses, I saw that even a prince of Egypt had a life that resembled a ride at an amusement park: sharp rises and deep falls. He went from the river to the palace, to murder, to exile, and from retirement to becoming an ancient world leader. What a ride! Why do I expect that my life should be level and smooth? A bigger question: How am I weathering the trip during the nerve-racking ups and terrifying downs?

◯ **Trust God to get you through it.** Heather shared this with me: "Two people may face the same disaster. One will seem to walk right through it, and the other will be destroyed by it. How a person responds all depends on *attitude*." Trusting God more is a quality of my faith. Is it also an attitude? Did Moses have a spiritual swagger when entering Pharaoh's court? . . . I can see it!

DAY 22

Pray

Read: Exodus 1–2

FROM MY JOURNAL

- Abraham's family grew into a nation. Life was bitter for the Israelites, and Egyptian prosperity depended on their bent backs. Yet God's people grew mighty. I found myself asking, "Which is harder for me: a life of ease or one with many challenges?" Trusting God more, I know you can survive both. Moses survived both a life of ease as part of Pharaoh's court and a life of challenge when wandering in the wilderness. The apostle Paul acknowledged that we can be thankful with much or little, in good times and bad, as long as the Lord strengthens us (Philippians 4:10-13). Give it a read.

- God's plan for Israel seemed to hit a brick wall for hundreds of years. In reality, God was keeping a promise to give Abraham as many children as the stars and to give the world a Savior from the bloodline of Israel! I find it interesting that the same river that was meant to take Moses' life was used to save him! In Pharaoh's court, God gave Moses a portion of the education he needed for leadership. God was shaping Moses even while he was separated from his birth family. I acknowledge that God shaped me with the people and experiences of my youth, both the good and the bad. Trusting more, I understand that the process is still ongoing. How is God shaping us today, and what's his purpose? Time will tell!

- Moses committed murder and ran for his life. After 40 years of pampering and royal splendor, he hid in the wilderness. God heard the groaning of his children in chains; remembered his ancient agreement with Abraham, Isaac, and Jacob; looked on the plight of his people; and felt concern as only the Father could. As a parent, I can relate to this and would be ready to protect my children. Get ready for divine action!

JOURNAL YOUR THOUGHTS

DAY 23

Pray

Read: Exodus 3–4

FROM MY JOURNAL

- Moses' education continued. He knew the wilderness. He lived there with sheep. Formal education was followed by practical instruction. A flock needs food, water, protection, understanding, and the guiding hand of steady leadership. In a simplified way, people's needs are identical to a flock's needs! I went to college and grad school, yet God shapes me for service by rubbing shoulders with his people, working at their side, and sharing their joys and woes. God makes leaders for family, church, and state. Am I the leader God wants me to be? needs me to be?

- The account of Moses and the burning bush is a wonderful example of God's intervention on behalf of the people he loves. He is holy, pure, and sinless, yet he approached Moses at work and gave him a new mission! Moses was to lead Israel out of Egypt to the border of the Promised Land. I understand Moses' insecurity and fear in accepting God's call to service. Don't you love it when Moses ran away from his staff when it turned into a snake?! He was a chicken—like me jumping at the sight of a garter snake! Haven't I felt the same way as Moses? Haven't I made excuses as to why service to God is impossible? Moses has got nothing on me! But with the task comes greater trust as God promises to go with me and empower me. This gives me a boost. How about you? Great trust reaches out a hand, at God's command, and grabs the snake by the tail!

JOURNAL YOUR THOUGHTS

DAY 24

Pray

Read: Exodus 5–6

FROM MY JOURNAL

- It grows darker before the storm. Taskmasters demand quotas met, even as bricks are made without straw provided. I'm retired, but you may not be. Is your workplace a testing ground for trust? I know it is. I used to come home feeling beaten down. I need to remember not to blame when God asks me to patiently trust.

- *Impossible* has got to be God's favorite word, just before heavenly power comes to the rescue. The stage is set for the drama of Exodus to unfold. God announced deliverance, even when his people failed to have the eyes to see it. Moses started to doubt. Critics and naysayers have a way of breaking down my trust too. Will I listen to God or the mob? I found Exodus 7:1 interesting. Aaron and Pharaoh were supposed to listen to Moses and hear . . . God! When I listen to Moses, am I listening to God?

JOURNAL YOUR THOUGHTS

DAY 25

Pray

Read: Exodus 7–8

FROM MY JOURNAL

- God stirred up Moses' courage even as he hardened Pharaoh's heart. Moses was moved to listen, believe, and obey, while Egypt's king did the very opposite. If people reject God, eventually the Almighty will give them their way and his judgment. Imagine, having miracles from heaven right before our eyes and yet turning

a deaf ear to the Lord! From this preserve me, Father in heaven! To reject God is to ask for trouble that may end up being eternal.
- God gave Moses the power to turn water into blood and plague the land with frogs. How did Pharaoh's magicians duplicate the miracle? They used "secret arts" (Exodus 7:11), lying trick of the devil. I never want to forget that the devil is mighty. However, he is not *almighty*. Only our God can reverse the disaster he has sent. Also, notice that the magicians with their dark arts cannot make dust into gnats. They confess, "This is the finger of God" (Exodus 8:19). Hell can go so far and then no farther! When flies devastate Egypt, God's people and the land of Goshen are spared! Deliver me, Lord! I put my trust in you!

JOURNAL YOUR THOUGHTS

DAY 26

Pray

Read: Exodus 9–10

FROM MY JOURNAL

- The plagues continued: livestock died, boils festered, hail accompanied by lightning terrified and destroyed, locusts devoured, and darkness blanketed the land. The citizens of Egypt suffered all of it. I carefully read and noticed that although God's children were exempted from the majority of these plagues, it looks like they had to endure the boils and the locusts. Wow! May I be asked to suffer if God chooses to teach my country a lesson? Will I trust that God is right in whatever he chooses? Will I thank him for sparing me most of the pain, even if I must endure some? Will I trust God even more?
- Pharaoh was trapped under God's judgment. The heart that Pharaoh hardened, God now also hardened. The end was coming for Pharaoh, even as Israel anticipated an end to slavery. I can sense

it. If I saw God bring a world power to its knees, nine times over, would I recognize what happened and trust him with my future? Would I entrust him to deal with all my enemies?

JOURNAL YOUR THOUGHTS

DAY 27

Pray

Read: Exodus 11–12

FROM MY JOURNAL

- The tenth plague was the closer. The enemies of God's people were broken. The Israelites would loot the land and leave captivity with their own families and new possessions. The blood of the Passover lamb protected believing families, and God's children were spared the loss of their firstborns. It is not an accident that God's Son is called the "Lamb of God" (John 1:29) and our "Passover lamb" (1 Corinthians 5:7). God's anger with our sin passes us by as we hide behind Jesus' blood. Cover me and my family, precious Savior! I trust the blood of the Lamb makes the difference!

JOURNAL YOUR THOUGHTS

DAY 28

Pray

Read: Exodus 13

FROM MY JOURNAL

- The Lord commanded the people to remember what he did with the tenth plague. The Passover would be a yearly feast, and the firstborn males of the family, flock, and herd would belong to the Lord.

Families were instructed to redeem firstborn sons. They *redeemed*, that is, "bought back," every firstborn animal or destroyed it. I am a firstborn son. I am redeemed with Jesus' blood. Do I belong to the Lord? Yes, and you do too!

- God knows his people and plans, in advance, the course they will take. He led them away from war and to the sea. No shortcuts. No detours in God's plans. God led them where he wanted them. Trusting God more, do I give him the same credit in my life?

JOURNAL YOUR THOUGHTS

Does it seem like you are trusting God more? Sometimes I feel the progress or see its proof. Most often, I just know I still believe and need spiritual strength to grow. It's like working out at the gym. I'd like to be "ripped" after a week, but mostly I'm sore. I feel a little healthier. I'm making healthy choices and trusting it will pay off!

Twenty-eight days down . . . only 152 to go!

Promises Kept: Trusting God With the Road Ahead

I took a break from my 180. In the week that passed, I worked on my fields and gardens and went fishing on Lake Michigan. God was with me! Should I expect less? My equipment stayed in one piece, a rarity on my little farm. The saying goes, "If it doesn't break, you aren't farming!" In addition, I caught three salmon and one rainbow trout. Faith was having fun. And that is how it should be.

My trust is a part of me when I work, play, and especially as I try to write a book. I think we often view our trust in the abstract as if it is a detached characteristic we possess but not a vital part of our being like a heart or a brain. What if we gave faith the same attention that we give the rest of our bodies? How many hours a day do I feed, bathe, work, exercise, entertain, and rest my body? There are parallels. Faith is fed by Jesus' promises, cleansed in his blood, clothed in his rightness with the Father, exercised as I live my convictions and flex my trust in times of trouble, and given joy and rest in heartfelt worship. To my faith, trusting is like breathing!

But what do I trust? What is always true and never misleads me? What do I believe that I would stake my life on? my eternity on? What is the authority that instructs faith and directs me in what to believe and what not to believe? I do not assume we all will answer those questions in the same way right now. I pray we all might someday. I pray this chapter helps.

I'm certain you have picked up on it. I tipped my hand from the very beginning of our time together. I believe God's promises are true. God always keeps his Word to me, and that causes my trust to grow. I trust he gave me his Word to help me. I trust in a one-of-a-kind book, written over 1,500 years by about 40 writers. Although the authors were very different (backgrounds, circumstances, cultures, and languages), the message of their combined effort is perfectly unified. This could not happen by chance. An eternal hand guided the process. Their combined works are a library that records God's love and will throughout the ages. Love made promises, and a perfect God didn't break one of them! Love gave commands, and a loving God is serious about all of them! God is in his Word and keeps his Word! I trust the message of the Bible. And as I read the Bible, God does wonderful things inside of me. The Holy Spirit grabs my heart.

Through the Bible, the Holy Spirit inspires me to trust him in kind of the same way I win the trust of my grandchildren. I promise my Goofy Girl that we are going for french fries (her all-time favorite) after school. She is all smiles as I pick her up from preschool and buckle her into her car seat. I no sooner get myself in the Subaru and she asks with a happy glow, "Are we going to McDonald's for french fries?"

I ask right back, "What do you think?"

Her face lights up. "Yes!"

Why is she so sure? We haven't driven anywhere yet. We're still in the school's parking lot. We can't smell fried food. We can't see the restaurant. There is no decorated meal box sitting next to her on the seat. Yet she is certain she'll be enjoying those golden goodies minutes from now. Why does my darling girl sparkle with anticipation? She got a promise. And to her, that promise has authority. She knows who made her that promise: Goofy Grandpa. She knows I have the power to make good what I pledged. She knows she has my heart. She believes me when I tell her, "I love you." She knows my promise carries the authority to deliver. She has confidence when she has my word.

Flip the coin, and the same love and authority can carefully discipline or even choose to withhold a blessing. Think about some examples of when the Israelites questioned God's authority (see Numbers 11). When authority is questioned, sometimes the person in authority has to respond accordingly to offer an opportunity for reflection and repentance. My granddaughter knows this too. Ask her about the time she terribly misbehaved at McDonald's. I gently took her by the hand, carefully repacked her meal, and threw it in the garbage can as she watched. We walked back to the car, and I asked, "Do you understand what just happened?"

She said, "I'm sorry, Grandpa."

I got teary and said, "Me too. Let's go home for a peanut butter and jelly sandwich."

Do you have the heart of Jesus' Father? The gospel (good news) message of the Bible tells me I do. It has the authority to convince me. He loves me, and deep inside I am sure that is true. I don't deserve his love, never have and never will. Yet he has made me the apple of his eye, his cherished child, *because!* He loves you the same way. How do I know? *Because* . . . he didn't allow his eternally dear Son to be nailed to the cross just for me! At all costs, Jesus came to rescue you! How dearly does the Father love you to sacrifice his only Son to save you? Do you want your trust in him to grow? Then start with his promise of love. He wouldn't lie to you. Look at who made the promise and how he backed his word with great personal sacrifice!

Now, move on to every other promise he has made to you, every fact he has shared with you, every command he issued to you, and every truth he has given to you. His Word has authority like no other! Recognize his love and power behind every message and every command or warning he gives. The more we hear his voice and the more faith clings to it, the more trust grows no matter what God tells us. He is in his Word! The Word has authority!

Think back over our readings of the past four weeks. A loving God interacted with the people of this earth. He walked and talked to Adam and Eve in the pristine garden his power created. God's intent from the beginning was for a relationship and dialogue with us. He communicated promises and warnings, both of which were for the good of his creation. After sin infected our first parents, God still lovingly conversed with the fallen couple and promised a Savior. God talked to Cain and warned him against murder. God spoke to Noah, Abraham, Sarah, Jacob, and Moses.

I'll admit that their reactions varied. Unbelief rejected God's revelation. Think of Cain's response to God. Or think of the folks not on the ark after 120 years of urging! But faith received the message and recognized its authority. Hammers pounded to build the ark. Doubt smirked. Sarah was caught in the act. Yet an old man made love to his postmenopausal wife, and a child was conceived. Jacob, an exile, took his large family back home, and he reconciled with the twin brother he had deceived long ago. And Moses, a former prince turned shepherd, went toe to toe with an ancient world power! Every time the Bible mentions these conversations, every time it is recorded that "the Lord said," there is a pull on faith to do something. To believe the message. In the Bible, God says he is talking to us! Reject that? Smirk at it? No, believe this really happens, and trust the revelation of God's Word and its authority over faith!

TIPS ALONG THE WAY

◊ **Trust is fed and grows by God's promises.** Faith must do something, must react, must respond to what Scripture claims about itself:

2 Timothy 3:16-17: "*All Scripture* is *God-breathed* and is useful for teaching, rebuking, correcting and training in righteousness, so that the servant of God may be *thoroughly equipped for every* good work." I ponder: "*All* of the Bible? God breathed it all? Is it enough to teach me everything God wants of his servant?"

2 Peter 1:21: "Prophecy *never had its origin* in the human will, but prophets, though human, *spoke from God* as they were *carried along by the Holy Spirit.*" I consider: "Humans . . . through whom the living God speaks. God the Holy Spirit is *directing* the process as he carries them to deliver God's message!"

John 17:17: "Sanctify them by the truth; *your word is truth.*" Jesus my Savior made this promise! God's Word—all of it—is true!

2 Timothy 3:15: "From infancy you have known the *Holy Scriptures,* which are *able to make you wise for salvation* through faith in Christ Jesus." I've got this one! Why do I believe it at all? Why do I trust in Jesus as my Savior? Why do I trust the authority of Scripture, not only to save me but also to direct my faith? Because the Scriptures are able to make me wise for salvation. They feed my trust!

◊ **Ask others how God's promises have impacted their trust.** I've seen the power the Bible has on me. Look around. Do you see how the Bible has worked powerfully in the lives of others? Talk to them about it. Has the Word helped them fight addiction? depression? Has Scripture had a positive effect on their lives? Has it comforted them in the face of death? Think, "Power!"

◌ **God's commands also call for trust.** Try to remember some of the commands God gave his children so far in our Bible readings. In your journal, list as many as you can. I paged back through Genesis and Exodus and took a tally. I stopped counting at 25. When God commanded, faith was asked to trust more and more! What should I trust if God gives me a command?

During the following seven days, our readings will jump from Exodus to the books of Numbers and Deuteronomy. In the intervening chapters, many laws are given to God's Old Testament people that are not required of us in the New Testament. Jesus kept the entire Old Testament law for us. The Father wanted these commands obeyed perfectly. That's why his perfect Son needed to accomplish it! Jesus asks us to obey the law of love. In his teachings, Jesus restates the moral truths of the Ten Commandments, which he summarizes as "love God" (Commandments 1–3) and "love your neighbor" (Commandments 4–10).

DAY 29

Pray

Read: Exodus 14–15

FROM MY JOURNAL

- God's people panicked, blaming leadership rather than their own failure to trust! I am such a frightened man. Racked with fears. Like the Israelites, I sometimes want to hide back in the good old days. The Israelites seemed to have forgotten that the good old days were filled with the misery of slavery. My memory can also erase past miseries and how God got me through them, especially when I am struggling to trust. What is true for me is true for you. Your 180 has you leaving that slavery behind as you wait for the Lord to work your deliverance.

- The Red Sea split apart like a ripe melon by God's powerful command. Moses had authority because God's Word has authority! It has power over God's people too! Would we leave high ground and walk between walls of water? What if God commanded it? God protected his children against impossible odds. All the power of Egypt was destroyed on the same path that led Israel to safety! God loves what critics consider a long shot. That's why he bet on the Israelites . . . and me! He makes us winners! Sing your praise without a relapse of grumbling. See the miracle that turns the bitter sweet!

JOURNAL YOUR THOUGHTS

DAY 30

Pray

Read: Exodus 16

FROM MY JOURNAL

- "What's for dinner?" The people again grumbled and feared starvation. When will the drama stop and the new norm become trusting more? God rained his generous gifts of food and delivered meat for the table at twilight. During a time when I was serving as a "starving" missionary, God repeatedly proved to me and my family that he faithfully provides exactly what we need. One look at me and you'll know I didn't miss a meal in the "wilderness"!

- Why didn't God want his children to hoard manna? Why gather every day and only gather extra before the Sabbath? Why did Jesus teach me to pray, "Give us today our *daily* bread"? I worry too much. It works against a carefree, generous life that trusts God more every day. Yes, there is a place for due diligence at work, just like the Israelites gathering manna and quail. But I still need to trust God for food every day.

JOURNAL YOUR THOUGHTS

DAY 31

Pray

Read: Exodus 17–18

FROM MY JOURNAL

- "Is the LORD among us or not?" (Exodus 17:7). Wait, what? The Israelites saw the pillar of cloud and fire each day and night. They witnessed the glory of the Lord descending to earth. They ate bread from heaven, drank water from solid rock, walked through a sea, and experienced plagues that broke their chains, yet they could say this? Walking by sight is not walking by faith. Faith believes in the unseen. Aaron and Hur held up the prophet's hands. Joshua fought the battle. But the altar proclaimed the truth: "The LORD is my Banner" (Exodus 17:15).

- When talking to his father-in-law, Moses stated the facts but did not take any credit. His story is about "how the LORD had saved them" (Exodus 18:8). Where's my power to navigate the struggles of life? Trusting more will mean giving God the credit because he deserves it. Faith gives God his due.

JOURNAL YOUR THOUGHTS

DAY 32

Pray

Read: Exodus 19

FROM MY JOURNAL

- At Mount Sinai, the people were ready to receive God's dos and don'ts. They were commanded to obey, or disaster would strike. The thunder and lightning, the thick cloud and smoke, the trembling of the earthquake, and the sound of trumpets blaring emphasized God's power and majesty. The people were to take God's Word seriously. They trembled. Do I still tremble when God speaks? Does trusting more demand a healthy fear that God really means what he says?

- Only Aaron was allowed to go with Moses to receive God's commands. Through faith in Jesus, we are privileged to approach God also (Romans 5:1-2). I must first go in faith to Mount Calvary's cross, where Jesus died for my sins, before I go to Mount Sinai and its commandments. Don't be surprised that after hearing the moral law of the Ten Commandments, we run back to the place where Jesus died saving us!

JOURNAL YOUR THOUGHTS

DAY 33

Pray

Read: Exodus 20

FROM MY JOURNAL

- "God spoke all these words" (Exodus 20:1). Some think the Ten Commandments are just suggestions of how we might live and not demands of what God expects. God spoke. I need to be honest as I read this and take to heart what God says. As I do, I tremble like ancient Israel. I haven't kept a single commandment perfectly. The people of Israel knew what they deserved in the light of the law: "Speak to us yourself [Moses] and we will listen. But do not have God speak to us or we will die" (Exodus 20:19). The Ten Commandments prove that I need Jesus and the forgiveness he freely gives. The law exposes my sin (Romans 3:1-20). God is holy. I am not.
- God commanded sacrifices on a simple altar to calm trembling hearts. Those sacrifices were a preview of a perfect offering God would make on a simple cross. The Lamb of God was slain for me!
- God used Moses to transmit his commandments to us. Did you know that Moses penned the first five books of the Bible while giving credit to God as their author? See the power of God behind the writings of Moses and all the authors of Scripture. This is why the Bible is God's Word.

JOURNAL YOUR THOUGHTS

DAY 34

Pray

Read: Numbers 11; 13:16–14:25

FROM MY JOURNAL

- In Numbers, we pick up the action after Mount Sinai. The people complained and God responded with consuming fire. When I complain to God (and I do), I need to recognize this angers him. Yet God the Father encourages us to humbly set our moans and groans before God and hide behind Jesus (Philippians 4:6-7). God does hear our complaints. Here he responded by giving Moses help at work and giving Israel tons of meat! Has God ever blessed me "until it comes out of [my] nostrils and [I] loathe it" (Numbers 11:20)? Do I even get sick of my blessings and complain about them too? How does God's response to my complaints lead me to trust more?

- Spies reported that the Promised Land was a land of bounty with not only plenty of resources but also plenty of enemies! Am I more inclined to trust the minority's faith or the majority's unbelief in my own life?

- In spite of all the miracles, guess which way the Israelites decided to go? Moses pled with God for mercy. He prayed for the forgiveness of heaven's wayward children. Moses reminds me of Abraham and his prayer for ten righteous people who might be living in Sodom and Gomorrah. God responded with grace and undeserved love, but in this case there were 40 years of consequences for faithless rebels. Have I ever had my own 40 years in the wilderness? I can recognize times in my life when I have been spiritually wandering, inconsistent in my faith. But through it all God has been consistently there for me, just like he was there for Israel. Dear Lord, spare me from any thoughts of wandering and move me to trust you more!

JOURNAL YOUR THOUGHTS

DAY 35

Pray

Read: Deuteronomy 1–3

FROM MY JOURNAL

- The wandering was over! A new generation had grown up. And the people trusted God to deliver on his promises! He had been training them to do that for four decades. If I seem to be wandering in life, my God has the power to bring me home. Trust! And keep walking in the direction he leads.

- No need for spies this time. A quick history lesson reminded the believing Israelites to move when God said, "March!" They were guaranteed success because they trusted and obeyed. I remember times when my disobedience brought me pain and disappointment. I also remember times when trusting God and obeying him resulted in me being blessed. My God is a loving Father. When he commands or promises, it is meant for my blessing. Life isn't easy, but it is easier when I trust he is with me *and* is talking to me!

JOURNAL YOUR THOUGHTS

Take 180 and subtract 35 . . . 145 days to go and you reach your 180! Are things starting to turn for you? Keep going!

Check Engine: Repentance Led by Trust

Another distraction from my 180: The engine light went on in my 1998 Ford pickup truck. It's an old truck but has been very dependable. I don't remember how many moves that F-150 facilitated. My kids depended on me and "Betsy" to haul them all over the Midwest. And now there is this little red, glowing image of an engine telling me I have trouble.

That light means I have to do something. I have to visit my mechanic. You don't ignore a warning light. It may signal something minor that is easily fixed. However, it could be telling you the truck is ready to conk out. So I took it right in. I sighed in relief to find out a sensor was bad, and my almost antique truck just needed a little tweaking and a $75 fix. Parts included!

The last section of Bible readings once again set off an alarm in me. My heart's warning light, aka my conscience, went on. All those commandments made the people of Israel tremble with terror. What scared them? If I didn't believe in the authority of Scripture or I made a joke of sinning, there would still be reason for pause at Mount Sinai. What if God is serious about his law? What if violators receive more than just warnings when they have exceeded God's limits? What if a God who empowers his promises also stands behind his promises to punish lawbreakers?

During my 180 I took time to review the Ten Commandments. I've taken similar spiritual inventories throughout my life. The law of

God tears the calluses off a heart that has the habit of hardening every day. My 180 showed me again what I've grown to expect. Were my attitudes, thoughts and fantasies, conversations, and daily activities in sync with what God expects? No. Am I in perfect running condition or am I just as broken as my truck? I can see the check engine light. Take the time. Review the Ten Commandments. Seriously consider what you see. Don't minimize what's broken. I couldn't.

Many churches use a catechism, a book of questions with Bible answers, for instructing their young people. Hey, let me tell you, the same little book helped me with my 180. I got out my copy of Luther's catechism and started my spiritual inventory. As you read the catechism, notice how Martin Luther weaves Bible references in with each response. Luther took a whole-Bible approach to understanding God's law. Luther viewed the commandments in the light of the New Testament. Restrictions God once imposed on Israel in the Old Testament were lifted from us in the New Testament by Jesus. Luther showed how God's love for us and our respect for God empower our obedience. Obedience to God demonstrates love back to God, especially by loving the people around us. Here is how that looks when we review the Ten Commandments:

1. **No other gods.** Love the triune God—Father, Son, and Holy Spirit—more than anyone or anything. If someone or something is more important to me than God, it has become my god.

2. **Honor God's name.** God has many proper names (Savior, Redeemer, Comforter, Lord, etc.), and each should be used respectfully and never foolishly. God's good name is his reputation. I should be careful what the world learns about God by my use of his name!

3. **Worship God.** He deserves it! Worship him publicly with other believers who hold faithfully to the Christian faith. And worship him privately at home. Your 180 is part of that personal worship time.

4. **Honor and obey God's representatives.** God has placed parents, teachers, employers, police, and government officials over us to bless us. Let's be a blessing to them!

5. **Protect life.** God gives life, and it is precious. Love life. Nurture life. Care for life. Do not diminish another person's life with words or actions. Do not destroy life unless God in his Word gives an exception (animals for food, self-defense, etc.).

6. **Protect marriage.** Marriage is a gift from God. It is the foundation for family and society. If I'm a married person, I must respect my marriage, and whether I'm married or single, I must respect the marriages of others. Sex is also a gift from God and is reserved for marriage, with no exceptions. And finally, God intended marriage to be between a man and woman, committed to each other for life. Loving God's gift means respecting God's gift.

7. **Protect property.** God gives me property and does the same for my neighbors. God, in wisdom, determines the levels of wealth that each person receives. And I am not to take what belongs to someone else, trusting that God has blessed me with enough to meet all my needs.

8. **Protect reputations.** No fake news about other people. No spins on the truth. No campaigns to distort what others think about me or those around me.

9. **Be content** with what you have. Watch feelings and desires! Do not want what God forbids you to have. Do not be envious, conniving, and manipulative by longing for someone else's belongings.

10. **Be content** with the lives entrusted to you. Watch feelings and desires! Do not let yourself want another

person's spouse, children, employees, or even pets! God forbids "wants" that violate his will.

I've broken all these commandments at one time or another. I am not proud of this. I'm honest. Go ahead: pick a commandment. Try and dodge the standard of love that God expects from you and me. Hold your behavior up to the standard of God's perfection.

As a child, I openly displayed examples of wrong thinking with my words and impulsive actions. Watch children in their unguarded play. Sometimes, they are brutal with one another. Sobs of broken hearts, teeth marks, and bruises on their playmates prove the point. They twist the incriminating evidence: "They started it!" "They deserved it!" "They hurt me first!" "I'd never do that, think that, or say that!" They demonstrate sinfulness without remorse followed by intentional cover-ups.

What has changed? As I became older and wiser in the ways of the world, I just became cleverer in my sinning. I can usually control outbursts of lovelessness and conceal from the public my true identity as a lawbreaker. If you'd see me, you'd think, "He's a nice guy. Polite. Happy. Obedient." It's a good thing you can't look at what I am thinking and feeling. The wickedness inside me is constant and strong.

Be honest. How would the opinions of others change if they knew what went on in our heads? What if they knew the real you and me? The person who is hidden and rarely surfaces but is obvious when we're behind the walls of our fortress of solitude? What I do, say, think, or feel when no one else can see is the real me! Oh, and by the way, the all-knowing God we worship always sees!

As a kid I'd go to church and join the congregation in publicly confessing my sins to God. This is a regular thing in many Christian worship services. I'd join my voice with others: "I, a poor miserable sinner, confess to you all my sins and iniquities with which I have ever offended you, and justly deserve your temporal [in real time, today] and eternal punishment." Did I feel miserable about my sin? Should I? Am I miserable about all my sins except for the ones I enjoyed and didn't get caught doing? Should I be punished? Is God really that angry because I sassed my mother? made my sister cry with my teasing? hit that kid who pushed me? cursed to be like the newsboys at the paper station? (I peddled the *Detroit News* seven days a week. So multiply that one to get the impact of how often God's name was misused.)

Think about these questions from ten-year-old me and compare them with the questions you ask in your everyday life. Ask yourself: Do I take sin seriously? When I sin, do I fear that I will destroy my relationship with my Savior and lose heaven? Would I rather do anything than spend time with God? Do I "damn" my way through the day? Is it a major chore to hear a sermon? Do I ridicule and put down my boss or government officials? Who did I hurt again today? Is sexual fantasy my entertainment and not confined to desire in my marriage? Did I cheat my employer by having someone punch out for me and leaving work early? Did I gossip or lie to save myself embarrassment? Do I harbor discontent, jealousy, and envy for everyone who seems to have an edge on me? Would I consider it overkill to say, "I, *a poor miserable sinner,* confess to you, Lord, *all* my sins and iniquities with which I have *ever* offended you, and *justly* deserve your *temporal and eternal punishment*"?

The Holy Spirit has convicted me and convinced me to confess my sins, all my sins, even the ones I have forgotten or don't remember committing. As this book is read, I'm certain it will reach people I have sinned against. I am so sorry, sincerely sorry, for the way I treated you. You deserved better, and God expected more from me. Forgive me, please. I confess my sin to you and to God. By God's grace and with his help, I'll be different the next time you see me. Different than what you remember. I ask Jesus to forgive me. And what makes the difference for me is that he has! That changes my life every day!

TIPS ALONG THE WAY

- **Repentance brings a change to our thinking.** To *repent* means "to have a change of mind." The sin we thought so desirable becomes detestable. God's power moves us to turn away from sin and make a 180 back to God's way of thinking.

- **Repentance has two parts: confession and trust in Jesus.** Confession of sin doesn't make up for my bad behavior. It acknowledges it. Trusting more has me believing God's condemnation of sin even more. Please, don't stop there though! If you do, it will drive you to despair. Trusting more must include believing that Jesus makes the greatest difference for sinners. Can you recite John 3:16? Jesus is God's Son given into death to erase our sin debt. Christ's blood washes the sin ledger clean. Trust this fact and you will not perish, but God will give you everlasting life because of what Jesus has done on our behalf!

- **Watch out for *proud* repentance.** The words are right, but the heart is wrong. Like a six-year-old forced to say, "I'm sorry," I can approach God believing that my sins are really the exception to God's law of love. Such confession is not from a broken and contrite (truly sorrowful) heart. It is haughty and views personal confession of sin as an obligation, not as an opportunity to humble myself before God and turn to him for forgiveness.

- **Christians still struggle with sin even after they repent.** It is a little frightening to replay incidents in my life. A friend of mine once said, "Right doesn't always mean righteous [right in God's sight]." Sometimes I was sure I was in the right. The words and actions may have appeared godly, but the attitude behind what was done or said was rotten to the core! I still have a sinful nature, a predisposed inclination to sin that lives inside of me. Like me, the apostle Paul also shared this experience. Read the confession of a man who called himself the chief of sinners: "I know that good itself does not dwell in me, that is, in *my sinful nature*" (Romans 7:18, emphasis added). But read what else Paul said in his full confession in Romans 7:14-25. Even in the middle of his personal struggle, Paul trusted in Jesus.

◊ **God gives us friends to help in the struggle.** Sometimes sin is so bothersome that my guilt crushes me. Privately, I confess all sins to God. However, if something I have done bothers me, even after I have privately repented, fellow Christians can remind me that even *that* sin was carried to the cross by our Lord. So find a trusted Christian friend or member of the clergy with whom you can talk confidentially. We don't need to punish ourselves with guilt. Jesus finished our punishment, just as he declared on the cross. It is true! Read John 19:17-30. Also, look up what Martin Luther said on confession in his catechism (*Luther's Catechism*, Northwestern Publishing House, 2017, pages 342-348, questions 337-345).

Our readings during the next seven days take us through the life of King David and to examples of the poetry he wrote. These song-poems are called psalms. See David as a repentant child of God.

DAY 36

Pray

Read: 1 Samuel 16–17; Psalm 3

FROM MY JOURNAL

- Saul was the first king of Israel. He was not a good example of being a follower of God. To put it bluntly, as king, Saul didn't follow, wouldn't follow, and completely gave up on following the Lord. The Lord eventually chose another king. He was none other than the great King David. A warrior, politician, musician, and poet, as well as handsome, strong, and healthy, David had it all. But more important, David was given a heart of faith and a deep love for the Lord his God.

- Young David slayed the enemy giant! He was an instant hero. Did you catch who was credited with the victory (1 Samuel 17:45-47)? I don't face my giant problems alone. I trust that God can provide simple alternatives (pebbles from the brook) and that he can successfully direct the outcome (bull's-eye!). When I overcome the ginormous, I also know who deserves the credit. As I trust more, will I see God's hand in my successes?

JOURNAL YOUR THOUGHTS

DAY 37

Pray

Read: 1 Samuel 18–20; Psalm 23

FROM MY JOURNAL

- After being blessed and given talent and ability, David became a victim of envy. Do the envious see their sin, or are they as crazy as King Saul? Do I recognize the green monster in my own heart?

Wanting what God forbids leads to action God forbids. I remember Jesus saying this to his disciples in Mark 7:20-23. Check it out!
- Believing friends are a great gift from God! Cherish them! David had such a friend in Saul's son, Jonathan. Jonathan not only gave generous gifts to David but also put his own life and future on the line for his friend. Jonathan was the heir apparent for the throne, yet trusting God more, he became the Lord's agent in protecting Israel's future king! As I remember this, I realize I need to stay in contact with believing friends.

JOURNAL YOUR THOUGHTS

DAY 38

Pray

Read: 1 Samuel 21–23; Psalm 13

FROM MY JOURNAL

- David was a fugitive living on the run. He took help where he could find it, where God gave it. Some paid a terrible price for doing what was right and good for young David. As I stand up for God's will, I may endure suffering and even death. I am trusting God for the courage to do this when the need arises.
- Narrow escapes are not as close as they seem when the Lord is engineering them. David made all the right moves to avert disaster, but God was the one blessing those plans. In the Lord's Prayer, we pray, "Deliver us from evil." We trust that God does this for others. Do we trust that our heavenly Father is doing the same for us?

JOURNAL YOUR THOUGHTS

DAY 39

Pray

Read: 1 Samuel 24–26; Psalm 14

FROM MY JOURNAL

- David did not return evil for evil. Saul was a spear-thrust away from being a problem solved, but David would not give the order. David recognized that God's prophet anointed Saul as king by God's direct order. Only God had the right to remove Saul from office. Great faith believes that God establishes governmental power and can depose it as he desires. I believe this but need to trust the Lord more as he works through local, state, and national politics. Would I be happier if I turned off the news and instead tracked God at work in changing history?
- A godly woman saved her husband from ruin and gave a future king God-pleasing advice. A woman like that is a treasure! After her first husband's death, Abigail married David. I thank God for my "Abigail," especially on the days I'm a "Nabal"!

JOURNAL YOUR THOUGHTS

DAY 40

Pray

Read: 1 Samuel 27–28; Psalm 19

FROM MY JOURNAL

- David lived as a double agent among the Philistines, who were ancient enemies of God's people. He pillaged and killed to provide for his little army. I don't like this. But I remember that God's Word records the truth whether I like it or not.

- Enemies of God's people were exterminated by a man God continued to love. I don't always understand how God works around sin and through troubling times. I guess that's why I need trust.
- The Lord no longer helped King Saul. Saul put his trust in mediums and spiritists. Like Pharaoh's magicians, this woman looked to the devil for power and answers. God used the situation to inform Saul of his ruin. I trust the Lord. Trusting God more means not turning to the occult or superstition for life's answers. Tear up the horoscopes!

JOURNAL YOUR THOUGHTS

DAY 41

Pray

Read: 1 Samuel 29–31; Psalm 32

FROM MY JOURNAL

- David and his soldiers did not raise a hand against Saul and the army of Israel. The Amalekites David had previously raided struck back at him. God used events to bring David home just in time to save his wives and the families of his men. God gave David success over his enemies and gave his soldiers back their wives and children. Do my actions ever put my family in danger? At times, I'm afraid they do. Prevent this, Lord, and protect my loved ones.
- Saul committed suicide, and his example encouraged another to do the same. I believe it would have been better for Saul to die at the hands of the Philistines than to take his own life. No matter how terrible the situation is, suicide is not the answer. I trust that my God can do all things. He works miracles against the odds. He makes everything possible. Trusting God more leads to turning away from quick and sinful fixes and trusting him for solutions.

JOURNAL YOUR THOUGHTS

DAY 42

Pray

Read: 2 Samuel 1–3; Psalm 38

FROM MY JOURNAL

- David mourned Saul and Jonathan's deaths. He ordered his people to do the same. David was anointed king over a 12th of God's people, and civil war broke out with the house of Saul. David's support grew stronger, and he wisely dealt with his conquered enemies. In every battle, there needs to be a time for the fighting to stop and peace to start. I recognize that the old battles in my life are over. I'm not under attack or attacking. Lord, grant peace!

JOURNAL YOUR THOUGHTS

Forty-two days of the experiment passed quickly. By my figuring, you are almost a quarter of the way to your goal. Grace is working!

Driving Forward: A Harvest Fueled by Trust

When I finger through the pages of my journals (I ended up with more than one!), I am amazed at how ordinary my life is. It reads like an endless "honey-do" list. I live on a farmette, which is a house, a pole barn, and a 20-acre backyard! I have endless chores and lots of broken or breaking machines. The high side of my God-given setup is the harvest: produce galore from a garden plot that houses cucumbers, squash of various varieties, tomatoes, green beans, asparagus, corn, onions, lettuce, and endless herbs. That same half-acre enclosure also protects what I lovingly call my "fruitatorium." (Try and find that in a dictionary!) Apple trees, pear trees, cherry trees, blueberry and raspberry bushes, and several healthy Concord grape vines promise pie, jam, jelly, juice, and, yes, our own mixed fruit wine. My critics will tell you it isn't that good unless a lemon-lime soda spruces it up. But if you have never had a taste of Berry-Cherry-Grape Misty Hallow wine, then you don't know what you're missing! God is so good to me! After the sweat and tears, he gives me a harvest. I have come to expect a harvest.

Should God expect any less from me and my repentance? By his grace, God turns me from sin, flips me around to see his face, and then smiles and welcomes me back into his forgiving arms. How many times each day is that the case? But wait! Then God, with the confidence of a loving Father and master gardener, looks for a harvest! Trusting him more, I live as he thinks best. I produce fruits of repentance: my 180!

Mixed in with fruits of faith are my fruits of repentance. They have to be. Fruits of faith are anything done out of love for God. Fruits of repentance are anything done out of love for God because he changed my thinking about sin. As a forgiven child of God, I hate sin and love to please him. Faith in Jesus is quick to promote that.

In John 15:1-17, the eternal Father trims dead wood off the vine. The gardener promotes growth and a harvest from new wood. Jesus is that vine. Nutrients and water flow from the soil through the roots of the vine to living branches ready to produce. We are the branches, grafted to the vine and secured there by faith. As long as all this is true, there is good news in the garden of our lives. Love and forgiveness surge from Jesus to us personally, and we will bear much fruit. This is only possible in Christ because without our Savior, "no branch can bear fruit by itself; it must remain in the vine" (John 15:4). That's true of tomato plants and also true in our life of faith. We stay connected to Jesus as we remain in his Word. And when you consider that the finest harvest from us is still scarred by faulty attitudes and sinful pride, the constant connection to Jesus is an absolute necessity. Our God creates the desire in us to do his will, empowers the doing, and cleanses what is done with the Savior's blood. Connected to Christ = harvest!

God's love pushes me to show love to him and people around me. The fruits of my faith are the finest things you see in me and the nicest things you know about me. And if you are around me long enough to recognize my sin and witness my repentance, you will see our God go to work again. You will see evidence that he is changing me. God the Holy Spirit influences my choices. "The acts of the flesh [the sinful state of human beings] are obvious: sexual immorality, impurity and debauchery; idolatry and witchcraft; hatred, discord, jealousy, fits of rage, selfish ambition, dissensions, factions and envy; drunkenness, orgies, and the like" (Galatians 5:19-21). That is me in sin. Now God works repentance. Look at me now! "The fruit of the Spirit is love, joy, peace, forbearance, kindness, goodness, faithfulness, gentleness and self-control" (Galatians 5:22-23).

You should read this whole section (Galatians 5:16-25) to appreciate what God does to all the branches of the vine. God's love moves me to say, "I'm sorry!" Don't stop there. God's love also moves me to ask, "What can I do to make it better?" First, there is repentance, but then, on its heels, is the fruit of repentance. God, the gardener, expects no less. Jesus' love for us will produce no less. Repentance means change . . . and nothing less!

TIPS ALONG THE WAY

◌ **When it comes to fruit, first ask WHJD and then WWJD.** This is not original, but it's helpful to me in my life of repentance. First, **w**hat **h**as **J**esus **d**one? He loves me and died in my place to make me his very own! True repentance always starts with Jesus. Then, **w**hat **w**ould **J**esus **d**o? In any given situation, think with the mind of Christ and imitate his life of loving service. This combination seems to me to be the right motivation and right direction for the fruits of repentance.

◌ **Fruits of repentance grow from trusting all that God's Word says.** You may have sensed this spiritual change in yourself: (1) God's law makes us aware of our sin, and our conscience tells us the law is right and we deserve the punishment it threatens. (2) God's gospel moves us to hide in God's love, to openly confess our sins, and to trust that Jesus was punished for what we have done. (3) The gospel with its message of love picks us up and nudges us to look at the law in a new way: it is our guide for ways to please the Lord. So the idea of making amends after sinning is a biblical concept. Amends do not earn forgiveness, but they do show our thankfulness for being forgiven.

◌ **Fruits of repentance are fueled by God's love and forgiveness.** Forgiveness is a gift that God or others give to me. Fruits of repentance are a gift that I give back to try and soften the effects of my sin. But what do I do if I have sinned, and although God forgives, people won't? Remember, forgiveness is never earned; it is a gift. And fruits of repentance should not be used as tools for manipulation. But the fruits of repentance can be a way to prove my sincerity after repentance. Sometimes the people I hurt need a track record of kindness toward them before they are ready to trust and forgive me again. Since God has already gifted me his love and forgiveness, I'm ready to bear that fruit.

◌ **God's Word helps me see which fruit of repentance is needed.** I don't have to rack my brain to determine the right "fruit" for the right occasion. Identify the behavior that hurts God or other people, and the right fruit is usually doing the opposite. Martin Luther once suggested that we should regularly review the Ten Commandments to develop sensitivities that are like the Lord's. He also suggested that believers should inspect the areas of service they are responsible for fulfilling: What kind of spouse have I been? Parent? Employee? Citizen? Teacher? Pastor? Church member? Do you get the idea? Forgiven by Jesus, we become happiest when we know he will be happy.

Join me in learning from King David. You will witness his life of repentance and the fruit that came from it. I'm ready! Let's do this!

DAY 43

Pray

Read: 2 Samuel 4–6; Psalm 69

FROM MY JOURNAL

- There are always people who will think it is to their advantage to hurt you when you are down. Saul's dynasty was history and then murderers went after his family. King David was above this and punished those who preyed upon the weak. Do I know someone being bullied? Do I take advantage of the weak? Would fruits of repentance make me look like David?

- Once again, David gave credit to God for victory over his enemies. As he tried to establish his capital as a place of worship, disaster struck! A man died for touching the ark of the covenant. Uzzah may have meant well when he reached out his hand to steady the ark. But to an unknowing observer, his actions may have looked like he was just dealing with an ordinary piece of furniture. The ark of the covenant was a piece of sacred furniture where God chose to make his presence known and his glory seen. Could Uzzah's actions, intentional or unintentional, have led someone to think that this piece of furniture was just another lifeless idol that needed help to keep from falling over? Do you ever think you have to help God out so that he doesn't fall on his face? Uzzah did and it turned out to be a bad move.

- Check out 2 Samuel 6:11. God blessed Obed-Edom for turning his home into a place where God and the ark were the center of attention and respected by all. Interesting. My home is blessed when it is God-centered!

JOURNAL YOUR THOUGHTS

DAY 44

Pray

Read: 2 Samuel 7–9; Psalm 61

FROM MY JOURNAL

- King David was not allowed to build a temple for the Lord. A future son of David would build it after he succeeded his father to the throne. David was not put off by this news. Instead, he broke into a prayer of praise, recognizing that God can bless as he chooses. Praise God for his grace!
- "The LORD gave David victory wherever he went" (2 Samuel 8:14). Did the success go to his head? No. David acknowledged the Lord and made offerings to his God. He also remembered an old promise to a friend and honored it. David cared for Jonathan's family. Honor your promises! Show kindness to others. When I haven't, I repent. What would the fruit of that repentance look like?

JOURNAL YOUR THOUGHTS

DAY 45

Pray

Read: 2 Samuel 10–12; Psalm 51

FROM MY JOURNAL

- David was blessed with victory over his enemies but personally lost a battle with temptation. King David became a Peeping Tom, an adulterer, a liar, a manipulator, and a murderer. Notice how one sin leads to another. I have experienced similar slow-motion train wrecks with sin. Thank God for his intervention!
- For a time, David wandered far from the Lord. The Lord went searching after him! Notice David's reaction to the prophet Nathan's

revelation: "I have sinned against the LORD" (2 Samuel 12:13). David was forgiven and yet there were consequences for his behavior. Consequences demonstrate how terribly destructive sin is. They give me an opportunity to learn from the experience and avoid temptation. They remind me that God's grace did intervene, and it is greater than my sin. David's acceptance of God's will was a fruit of his repentance. Help me, Lord, to grow from the consequences I endure.

JOURNAL YOUR THOUGHTS

DAY 46

Pray

Read: 2 Samuel 13–15; Psalm 25

FROM MY JOURNAL

- Look back at 2 Samuel 12:10-23. David's sin scarred his children and brought him pain throughout the remainder of his life. Is it God's fault when my sin rewrites his plan to bless me? I need to trust God more when nagging irritations follow me in life. I need to be honest with myself. Am I the primary source of what troubles me? A harvest of repentance may result in clarity and give me a better understanding of myself and my life.

- Absalom conspired against his own father and overthrew David's government. As David and his allies ran for their lives, God still provided friends who worked for his cause. Hushai, David's confidant, was one of God's agents sent to protect him. Who are my trusted friends? They are the ones who stand by me when the world seems against me. I need to appreciate them always and see them as gifts from heaven.

JOURNAL YOUR THOUGHTS

DAY 47

Pray

Read: 2 Samuel 16–18; Psalm 37

FROM MY JOURNAL

- Don't be surprised when someone receives pleasure from your pain. Identify the men who took advantage of King David's misery. Does anyone ever take advantage of your misery in a similar way? Commend such people to God. He has the wisdom and righteous judgment to level the playing field and make all things right. I trust you to do this, Lord. Change hearts or circumstances so that my situation serves you best.
- The civil war came to an end. The king's forces were victorious and the rebellion crushed. The victory was bittersweet. The kingdom was restored to David, but his dearly loved and rebellious son, Absalom, was dead. Trusting God more, I bow to God's will and appreciate King David's sensitivities. I should not gloat even when my enemies are destroyed.

JOURNAL YOUR THOUGHTS

DAY 48

Pray

Read: 2 Samuel 19–22; Psalm 31

FROM MY JOURNAL

- King David was restored to the throne, or so it seemed. More rebellion needed to be squashed for good order to return. A famine starved his kingdom for three years. When does the trouble end? Not in this world. Trusting God more, I call on him for help and wait for him to rescue me. He is a safe shelter for me to hide and my hope for deliverance.

- I really like 2 Samuel 22:30. With the Lord by my side, I cannot be outnumbered. Are there any obstacles in front of me? My God can lift me right over them in a single bound! Just like Superman!

JOURNAL YOUR THOUGHTS

DAY 49

Pray

Read: 2 Samuel 23–24; Psalm 54

FROM MY JOURNAL

- At the end of his days, David reflected on his life and his rule. Grace made him a God-fearing king. And God's everlasting covenant made him certain of his salvation. King David acknowledged God in his successes. God promised David his blessing and delivered on that promise. The great line of kings from David would stretch through the ages to the everlasting King, Jesus Christ our Lord.
- After this acknowledgment, sinful human nature turned David in the wrong direction. He started counting on his own strength instead of depending on the Lord, his strength. He counted his army and assessed his political power. He angered God. David was conscience-stricken and asked for forgiveness again. I know how this works: I praise the Lord in worship, but I can't make the ride home without needing forgiveness again. Repentance and the fruits of repentance are a way of life for God's believing children. They fill my day. They fill my years. This must try God's patience, but it leaves me appreciating his love.

JOURNAL YOUR THOUGHTS

You are now more than a quarter of the way through your 180. Take inventory. Journal about your growing trust in the Lord. I pray that you see buds on the branch of the vine!

Giving Directions: Pointing Others to the Way Ahead

My wife got her way. She had been searching the web for a new dog. The local humane society had a selection of purebreds that had been rescued from a puppy mill. Just gorgeous animals that were four years old, had been confined to a cage, and had pumped out as many puppies as their poor systems could handle. I wasn't sure these beautiful animals even knew their names, let alone ever been taught a single command. We didn't find the dog we were looking for. We wanted an inside dog, with known social skills (we have nine grandchildren), and I was hoping for one that was house-trained. The volunteers were very helpful but did not recommend a single puppy mill dog for our home. I'll admit, it was a disappointing ride home from the shelter. When I got home, I penned those thoughts of disappointment in my journal that night.

For some reason, maybe because of my disappointed mood, I wanted readings more uplifting than Old Testament history. That night I turned to Matthew's gospel and never turned back. I read through the rest of the New Testament to complete my 180. I wanted unveiled examples of Jesus' love. I wanted God's Son to grace my life with miracles. I wanted to review Bible accounts I had learned in Sunday school to see if an old believer could once again approach life with childlike faith.

As I spent my nights reading, my better half continued canine research and discovered a rescue organization called Sandi Paws. The group saves dogs from bad situations and captures feral puppies living on the streets.

The dogs receive medical treatment, are spayed or neutered, and are put into a home setting for foster care in the state of Alabama. Every so often the volunteers would bring a truckload of their orphans to a fairground and let you take a pet for a test-drive. After church that Sunday, we headed to Fond du Lac, Wisconsin, to check it out.

My wife saw a picture of the dog she thought she wanted. In a penned enclosure, we sat with this little wild knucklehead (the dog, not my wife). This puppy was off-the-wall. But over in the corner sat her beautiful, tan big brother. He looked like Old Yeller and was frightened by the circus of events surrounding us at the fair. I asked if we could take him for a walk and proceeded to put a collar on his neck attached to a rope leash. He didn't resist. I petted his ears. I ran my hands over his muzzle without a nip or a growl. We got out of the arena and a good-natured energy filled his body. I had him heel, and he didn't do half bad. I gave him a little lead. He went right for a bunch of scrubby bushes by the building, stopped, and then poked his head in the foliage. He startled a hen pheasant. At that moment, we both knew . . . we had found our dog. We named him Hogan, "Hogey" for short. He is as smart as he is handsome. He has the potential to be the best dog we have ever owned.

Wasn't that fun? I can talk to you about a house pet with the ease and humor of one friend to another. It is effortless. Easy!

Now, you'd think it would be just as easy to talk about my Savior as it is to talk about the dog. You'd be wrong. My life of faith would prove that. As a younger man, wearing loud bell-bottom pants, I'd break into a cold sweat whenever it was time to talk about J-e-s-u-s. I'd try a memorized gospel sales pitch I read out of a book, and I have to gratefully admit that the Holy Spirit didn't fail me. I got the words out and even managed to get the Word to the ears of people who needed Christ as much as I did.

Much older now, and literally thousands of experiences later, I don't really plan what I will say to folks not blessed to know our Lord yet. I trust more in God's power alone to convert a heart. I listen more, trusting God will show me how to help other spiritual victims learn about their rescue. I speak more of Jesus' love for them and what he did on the cross to save me and all people. God gives me opportunities every day to talk about the Savior. As easily as I can tell friends, relatives, acquaintances, and neighbors about the dog of my life, I now talk about the One who died for me and rose again to save my life now and forever.

This is not to say I haven't needed encouragement along the way. Several times during my 180 I crossed paths with a dear friend. He has journeyed with me through high school, college, and right up to today. He stood up at my wedding and I returned the favor for his wedding. I don't get to see him as much as either of us would like, but we call back and forth and send each other Christmas greetings. He's a busy guy. (I usually get his Christmas letter sometime in March!) But my friend has been a nonstop inspiration when it comes to a simple faith in Jesus that must tell everyone about his Savior. Jesus' name is on the stationary for his notes and fills the message on his answering machine. He even printed a business card that he leaves with his generous tip at the restaurant. He has something better than a 20 percent tip to share with the waitstaff: Money is only valuable for a moment, but heaven is gold forever!

Would you like to meet him? God uses him to revive my spirit in trusting more as I share Jesus more! My friend's name is Paul. When I first met him years ago, both of us were living away from home and just down the hall from each other on the second floor of our dormitory. As a ninth grader, he weighed 90 pounds and measured 4'10" tall. We were bound to be friends, fast and true, because I weighed 120 pounds and measured . . . (Did you guess it?) . . . 4'10" inches tall. We were two small people in a land of giants. All the girls were taller than us!

I'd like to directly quote Paul as he tells his story:

> I was blessed with a good mom. She knew how to spank her rebellious three-year-old. Then she taught me the Fourth Commandment: "Honor your father and mother that it may go well with you and that you may enjoy long life on the earth." I concluded I wouldn't be living long on the earth. This conclusion caused me to become very afraid of God, afraid of death, afraid of judgment day, afraid I'd be spending eternity in hell.

I was terrified every time the haunting question came to my mind, "Where will I be if I die?" Finally, during my junior year in high school, the Holy Spirit put that question in my mind again but then added the thought: "I think the answer is in John 3:16." I looked it up in my Bible. I read God's beautiful promise: "For God so loved the world that he gave his one and only Son, that whoever believes in him shall not perish but have eternal life." It didn't say, "Maybe"! I thought, "I believe in Jesus! Eternal life is mine!" For the first time in my life, I could go to bed at night and not be afraid of where I'd be when I opened my eyes! Then a better thought came to my mind: "I have to tell everyone I know about this!"

It seemed that whenever I was discouraged and bogged down in my faith, I'd hear from Paul. And his conversations would lift my spirits. With pure joy, he'd tell me he was learning Spanish! Sure enough, he had met a Hispanic family who didn't know their Savior.

Paul told me about an avowed atheist named Heinz. Heinz was living in the nursing home and was dying. He had thrown every pastor and person out of his room whenever they talked about faith. The nurses asked Paul if he would speak to him. Paul dove in and slowly became his best friend. He came to find out that Heinz had been a German prisoner of war in Siberia. After a visit or two, Heinz agreed to read the Bible with Paul. He started saying the Lord's Prayer in German. And he began remembering how he confessed the Christian faith on his confirmation day, back in the old country. That old man died, but not before repeatedly hearing that Jesus died for him too and rose again!

In another encounter, a man at a restaurant tried telling Paul a series of off-color jokes but ended up in a serious conversation about death. Now there's a change in conversation! The man was afraid, in his own words, "of shoveling coal for an eternity." Paul told him that through faith in Jesus, there would be no fire in eternity for him. The fire he deserved had been put out for good by his Savior!

The list goes on and on. Success is measured one soul at a time as God uses my friend to share a promise that he took to heart during his junior year in high school. "The answer is John 3:16!"

TIPS ALONG THE WAY

◊ **God uses ordinary people to do extraordinary things.** "You will be my witnesses," Jesus said in Acts 1:8. I know this is his will for me. I don't have a PhD. I'm not especially smooth or persuasive with my words. I don't try and talk people into Jesus. If I have a strong opinion about sports or politics, I'll tactfully but firmly let you know. If I had the cure for cancer, I'd find a way to tell the sick what I discovered. What would I do with a cure for death? I have that! So I talk about the Resurrected One. What I feel for Jesus fills my heart! Ask me. I'll tell you!

◊ **Make your plans, but trust God when he changes your plans.** I may plan when and where I will share my Savior. More often, I have found that God makes plans for me. I haven't always felt prepared. I'm in a situation and I know I should speak about Jesus. I know it, and too often I hold back. So I pray for even more opportunities and ask him to gear me up to use them because the time is right. I see God changing the plans of others too. One of my believing loved ones once told me, "Don't make me talk about Jesus to our family!" I said, "Okay, I will never make you." But in the face of loved ones dying, she speaks clearly, lovingly, and confidently about Jesus as the way to heaven. I don't make her. She wants to. She needs to, with all the fervor of a mother saving her child at the swimming pool!

◊ **God gives each of us a personal mission field.** Maybe I'm not some high-powered evangelist or missionary. I don't have to be anyone other than the person God has made me. I talk to children about Jesus in the Sunday school class I teach. I tell my grandchildren Bible stories. I try to help when I see spiritual danger in the lives of my children and my extended family. My neighbor just stopped in, and the conversation turned to Jesus. I confessed to my neighbor the things I don't know and can't understand. Then I shared the one thing I'm sure of (some days the only thing I'm sure of) and that is God's love for me in Jesus. Trusting more makes Jesus the center of my life. Like a bicycle wheel, Jesus is the hub, and everything connected to him spins around him. Conversation has a way of circling him.

○ **Think about who is included in telling *everyone* about Jesus.** Who do I talk to about Jesus? People who already know him need encouragement. People who have never really learned of him need knowledge. People who once loved Jesus but don't "friend" him anymore need to remember. People confused about the way to heaven don't understand that Jesus came to earth to save them. They can't save themselves from sin any more than they can save themselves from eternal death. Who do I tell about Jesus? Most everyone . . . unless they tell me to stop.

I hate change, but I do it anyway. I didn't start out too keen on getting another dog. It turned out well. I started reading the New Testament. Hey, I couldn't lose no matter what part of the Bible I studied. I really love the gospels. And I'm taking you along on my walk through the first four books in the New Testament. I'm also changing our study format . . . just a bit. I will still provide daily chapters or verses for study. We won't read a whole gospel, like Matthew, as a single book. I chose instead to focus on a certain event or subject and share what each of the gospels had to say. Be prepared to read from Mark one day, then skip to John, and end up in Luke. This is a lot of change. It will grow on you!

DAYS 50–56

Pray

Readings:

DAY 50	Luke 1	DAY 54	Luke 2
DAY 51	John 1:1-14	DAY 55	Matthew 3
DAY 52	Matthew 1	DAY 56	Mark 1
DAY 53	Matthew 2		

FROM MY JOURNAL

- Zechariah needs his own 180! I note the difference between his response to the angel's message and that of the virgin Mary. I want the grace to trust our God more so that I will stop being afraid and stop fighting his will for my life. My prayer is, to borrow Mary's words, "May your word to me be fulfilled" (Luke 1:38).

- It's Christmas! I compare John and Luke and watch the Creator become a real human being, born to be my brother, a part of my family. Thirty years went by in a snap, and quickly Jesus was a full-grown man entering his ministry. I highlight all the details of the Bible stories to help me tell them to my grandkids.

- I can't overlook the number of witnesses in these chapters. The Savior was the talk of the town: Gabriel, Elizabeth, Mary, and Luke all spoke about him. Luke investigated his gospel (Luke 1:1-4). Who do you think he interviewed for the manger story? There are also shepherds, Simeon, Anna, the boy Jesus himself, Magi (wise men), John the Baptist, the heavenly Father, the Holy Spirit, an impure spirit, and a man healed of leprosy. Did I forget anyone? I trust this truth: If people run into Jesus, there is someone they need to tell!

LOOK AT HOW THE PEOPLE IN THESE CHAPTERS WERE LED TO TRUST GOD MORE:

1. An untouched virgin bowed her will to a biological miracle (Luke 1).

2. This same, now very pregnant Mary traveled to Bethlehem on Caesar's whim and a prophet's promise. And as a new mother, she made do when there were no pajamas, cribs, or guest rooms (Luke 2).

3. Shepherds left their employer's profits in the field to visit a Savior in a feedbox. Then, these men who work the night shift shouted "good news that will cause great joy" whether the public listened or not (Luke 2).

4. A stepdad gave a newborn the name Jesus (which means "Savior") because an angel told him to (Matthew 1; Luke 2).

5. An old man waited a lifetime for a promise to be kept, and because it was, he was ready to die (Luke 2).

6. Magi made an incredible journey because the Scripture was true and the Christ was born (Matthew 2).

7. A man, woman, and child fled to a foreign land and were safe because that was what God desired (Matthew 2).

JOURNAL YOUR THOUGHTS

DAYS 57–63

Pray

Readings:

DAY 57 Luke 3	**DAY 61** John 1:15-51
DAY 58 Matthew 4	**DAY 62** John 2
DAY 59 Luke 4	**DAY 63** John 3
DAY 60 Luke 5	

FROM MY JOURNAL

- Through Mary, the bloodline of Jesus went back to Adam; read the genealogy in Luke chapter 3! In combat with the devil, Jesus fought using only God's Word, the same weaponry he has given me. The Word overcame Satan's heavy artillery (Matthew 4; Luke 4). Jesus spread the Word and healing happened (Luke 5) and a wedding was saved (John 2)! Reflecting on the power of Jesus' Word, I remember there are times I also need miracles: I have two unmarried sons in need of a spouse! I pray with confidence!

- Jesus is the Lamb of God: meek, mild, unblemished, and ready for sacrifice (John 1). Andrew was found by Jesus and found his brother Peter (John 1). Philip was called to faith and was used to call Nathanael to the Savior (John 1). Would God speak through me to reach the lost? Do I trust he'll give me the words and the ability to do it? He has.

- A learned teacher was taken to school by Jesus and taught that salvation (that is, being saved from hell and for heaven) is not performance-based but through faith in what God's Son did for him (John 3). I underlined and starred Christianity's favorite Bible verse.

JOURNAL YOUR THOUGHTS

DAYS 64–70

Pray

Readings:

DAY 64	John 4	**DAY 68**	Mark 3
DAY 65	Mark 2	**DAY 69**	Luke 6
DAY 66	John 5	**DAY 70**	Matthew 5
DAY 67	Matthew 12:1-21		

FROM MY JOURNAL

- Jesus had an appointment with a troubled woman at a well (John 4). He gave her the "living water," and she offered her whole town a drink! She leads them in asking, "Could this be the Messiah?" (John 4:29). Trusting more means sharing Jesus more.

- I thrill at the miracles! I believe they still happen, and I eagerly tell the stories of the paralyzed (Mark 2), the invalid (John 5), and the man with a shriveled hand (Luke 6) to those who are hurting. Those last two were healed on a day of rest, a day Jesus could have taken off work. But love filled Jesus and still does. A consuming need to help didn't allow him time to even eat! Does anyone ever think that I am "out of [my] mind" (Mark 3) because I work to help others for Jesus' sake?

- "Do to others as you would have them do to you" (Luke 6:31). As I trust more, I notice more about myself. My anger is volcanic. My outbursts are blistering. My resentment is unexplainable. As Jesus began the Sermon on the Mount (Luke 6; Matthew 5–7), I realized that buried deep inside me, the deadness of sin remains. I am very thankful that I have a Lord who raises the dead to a new life! Trusting more means living more like Christ. I am "salt" and "light" (Matthew 5).

JOURNAL YOUR THOUGHTS

DAYS 71–77

Pray

Readings:

DAY 71	Matthew 6	**DAY 75**	Matthew 11
DAY 72	Matthew 7	**DAY 76**	Matthew 12:22-50
DAY 73	Matthew 8:1-13	**DAY 77**	Luke 11
DAY 74	Luke 7		

FROM MY JOURNAL

- The wise person "hears these words of [Jesus] and puts them into practice" (Matthew 7:24). If I believe what Jesus says is right and good, then he expects I will do what he has told me. The Sermon on the Mount talks a lot about doing. What I do doesn't save me, but it is evidence that I believe in the One who has! I'd be wise to remember that.

- I meet the centurion again! Remember, I talked about him at the beginning of chapter 3. Now there's great faith and a demonstration of what more trust looks like. As I read identical accounts in the gospels, some details differ. This isn't a contradiction. As is true of all eyewitness accounts, there are different perspectives. The Bible writers see things from different sides of the street. When I put the details together, I see Jesus in 360-degree vision!

- Jesus loves the very people the world sees as unlovable. I'm glad. I'm numbered among them. I recognize his love even as he warns his enemies about their sins. If I can't see my hypocrisy, why would I need a Savior to forgive it? My Savior loves the wicked and hates their wickedness. He is repulsed by my sin yet claimed it as his own on the cross!

JOURNAL YOUR THOUGHTS

What do you think? These readings have you a third of the way home. Remember to pray, study, and journal. Ask your "W's." Stay the course to trust more!

The Road to More Trust Doesn't Need to Be Lonely

I have great news! My oldest daughter is expecting! She and her husband are very excited. And I am happy and anxious at the same time. My Rachel will be an older mother, not like Sarah and her Isaac (Genesis 21), but there are more risks with added age. This anxiousness is normal for me. I'm a protector for my clan. She belongs to my family.

More good news! My oldest son is getting married! Why am I surprised? Prayer works! And you want to know the kicker? My youngest son is bringing his new girlfriend to meet the parents! I need to ask for more miracles. That is a future chapter!

My heart is brimming with belonging! I have the gift of a good wife, five kids, three sons-in-law, at least one future daughter-in-law (maybe two), eight grandchildren, and another grandchild on the way. I am theirs and they are mine. This feels safe and comfortable.

I haven't always felt like I belonged. In fact, I have often felt like an outsider. Don't feel sorry for me. Some of it was my own doing, and some of it was beyond my control. Remember, I was short and round, which meant I was often the last one picked and easy to pick on. I grew up afraid to be home and easy prey for the fast and sleek on the streets. I was slow and lacked confidence. What kind of athlete do you think that made me? I liked just being on the team but found that fans hate anyone short of the winner, and the teammates don't think much of that either.

I was bright but not a brain. I could be friendly but didn't have many friends. I think I did okay with what I was given, but I never quite fit in.

Looking back, I can see that some of it was my own fault. When I felt shunned, I felt that an injury was done to me. *I should be loved and accepted,* I thought, *and that's not happening.* If others wouldn't let me into their group, then I'd imagine evil in their motives. I would hold resentment against those who "belonged." I would isolate myself from them, fortify my position against future attacks, interpret their overtures as hostile, and tailor my responses to give them a concrete reason for staying away and locking me out. See, I'm my own worst enemy. I sometimes contribute to my predicament. I guess I don't belong . . . at least, according to me.

I've met hundreds, no, thousands, who feel the same. They feel like the black sheep of their flock, like the plain among the gorgeous and glamorous, like the nerd surrounded by the popular, like a Simple Sam in the company of geniuses. They feel like an unwelcome visitor at their own alma mater or even their own church. I could make a franchise for all those who feel disenfranchised. And the situation seems to be getting worse.

I shared with you that I prayed my heart would be open to receive and my ears open to hear the people God would send my way. And I found the disenfranchised looked like:

1. A teenager brutalized by social media.

2. A homosexual feeling unwelcome at church yet welcoming a chance to grow in Jesus.

3. Four couples, all with Christian backgrounds and all but one person previously divorced, living together outside of marriage.

4. A mother of four, forsaken by Christian friends after a divorce where she was the victim.

5. A man divorced several times who was fighting drug and alcohol addiction.

6. A woman who sought counseling from her pastor, but the pastor did not address the problem, suggest additional appointments, or refer her for help.

7. A family suffering after a suicide.

8. Maybe . . . you.

Put all the particulars aside. I just focused on those with hurting faith, and in all cases, they had the feeling of being unwelcome with family, friends, or even the church. In some way, they all isolated and insulated themselves from a real, perceived, or imagined threat. In every case but one, the individuals had drifted from Jesus and felt distant or disconnected from Christ. That being said, they all still talked to me. And they talked about Jesus.

. . . I don't know how to fix this feeling. But I really want to. I know how dangerous it is to feel like an outcast. I believe the devil enjoys it when people feel alone and forsaken. I'm concerned because I recognize people with weak and wounded faith, and I can't get them out of my head. In one way or another, I love them all: family, friends, and neighbors. And I know I can do something to help. I could be around more to offer encouragement. I could give them a call or visit. I could offer them some support. But I feel limited. I don't always know whether others have made them feel like an outsider or if this is something they have done to themselves. And I can't always see the best way to help them. But I pray for them. I pray that Jesus would break down the barriers that keep loved ones apart.

I have a friend who is always there for me. Jesus loves me—more than that, he even likes me and enjoys hanging around me. He is not afraid of the mess that I live in, the mess that I make of my life. He's there when it is time for cleanup. Without him, it would never be cleaned up. He makes wise suggestions. He encourages the best in me. He is not looking for quick fixes but patiently applauds steady progress.

See him in Matthew 1:23. He is "God *with* us." He's not running to get away from me. He came to earth to be with me. He stays at my side, in good times and bad. When I read Matthew 12:18-21, I hear the prophet Isaiah describing me:

> Here is *my servant* [Jesus] whom I have chosen, the one I love, in whom I delight; I will put my Spirit on him, and he will proclaim justice to the nations. He will not quarrel or cry out; no one will hear his voice in the streets. *A bruised reed* [me] he will not break, *and a smoldering wick* [also me] he will not snuff out, till he has brought justice through to victory. In his name *the nations* [which includes me] will put their hope.

I've felt like a single reed ready to break, like a lone candle sputtering to stay lit. My friend Jesus didn't snap me off or snuff me out. He died, gave me justice, and rose from the dead to secure my victory. I am part of his family, whether I feel it or not. I can't be alone as long as I have him. He will help me when others leave me or if I imagine they have left me. I want to trust God more. My hope is in him. That's when I'm sure I belong!

TIPS ALONG THE WAY

- **I belong to Jesus' family simply because he loves me. Help others to know they belong too.** I hate the thought that any loved ones could do anything that would somehow place them out of my family. Treating family members like a hot mess helps no one. When communication stops and loved ones feel unwelcome on an occasion like Christmas, it really speaks against the reason for the holiday. God's Son was born a real baby to be with me. And with them. Love does so much more than ignoring them or sharing angry words and actions.

- **Think about who Jesus calls to belong to his family.** In our last series of readings, we read Mark 2:17. Jesus had dinner with the town's "sinners." He explains to his critics: "It is not the healthy who need a doctor, but the sick. I have not come to call the righteous, but sinners." First ask yourself: If a homosexual, a divorced person, an addict, and someone who had been bullied by social media because a family member committed suicide came to my house, would they be welcomed into my family? These are many of the reasons the people I talked to felt like outsiders. Then ask yourself: Would Jesus welcome them into his? Would Jesus welcome them because of who they might be or because of what he could do for them? I'm asking.

- **Love and growth take time and nourishment.** I believe that the highest form of love is to tell other victims of sin about their Savior. As they begin their life of faith, love slowly and carefully continues to share all of God's truth with them. Too much too fast and a young or wounded believer chokes, unable to take in all that a perfect God offers and expects. I look toward the future and gently care for the faith of others. We all need time, experience, and—most of all—ongoing nourishment from God's Word. Friends, I'm not there yet. I'm still longing to trust God more! Go easy on me.

◊ **Belonging means I want others to experience that belonging.** As I've gotten older, I have a heart for outsiders. I watch and recognize those who appear to be uneasy. At my church and in my home, I make a point to go to those who may feel like an outsider: the person fresh out of jail, the teen struggling with identity, the widow or widower, the one whose sin has just gone public, and the guest who seems uncomfortable and a little out of place. I smile. I introduce myself. I ask if I can help them. I listen for an opportunity to make them feel welcome. I'm not perfect at this. But each time I grow a little better. I believe I am trusting more when I'm not so quick to judge or give up on people. I keep trying to find those who feel orphaned by life. Sometimes God uses me to help. Sometimes he even uses me as a bridge for them to help welcome them back to Jesus' family. I'm not always smooth at this. I remind myself that I want to feel like I belong. I know they want the same.

I need to open the doors of my "fortification of isolation." (Oooh, I like how that sounds and hate how it feels!) Maybe I'm not being overlooked or slighted. Maybe I'm not being judged or rejected. Maybe I should take Jesus with me and just give my ex-spouse, estranged family, the classmates I think are being cold and heartless, and the church I see as condescending an opportunity to show they really do care about me like Jesus does. Wouldn't it be a kick if we all, in the end, thought we were chairman of the Disenfranchised Club? . . . Hey, I guess that means we belong together!

DAYS 78–84

Pray

Readings:

DAY 78	Matthew 13	**DAY 82**	Mark 5
DAY 79	Luke 8	**DAY 83**	Matthew 9
DAY 80	Matthew 8:14–34	**DAY 84**	Matthew 10
DAY 81	Mark 4		

FROM MY JOURNAL

- Jesus teaches with parables: everyday stories that contain a diamond of truth for believers. Read Matthew 13:11 carefully. The "secrets of the kingdom of heaven" belong to those who believe, which is why Jesus chooses to speak in parables. Some choose not to belong. They close their eyes, ears, and hearts to Jesus. Unbelief is a self-inflicted isolation from the true God. Jesus doesn't want this. His warnings are not just warnings. They are also invitations. Just think of Matthew 13:15: "I would heal them."

- I note several repeats of various parables. Memorable teaching that stuck in the minds of those who heard. In the parable of the sower and the seed, it is the seed, the Word of God, that works its own harvest. Forgive me, Lord, for being success-minded, statistically motivated, or "production proud" when I shared your Word. It is always you who makes good things happen . . . the harvest is yours!

I ALSO NOTE THAT I DO BELONG:

1. Luke 8:21—like family! Jesus loves me like his mother and as a brother!

2. Luke 8:26-38—even when others want nothing to do with me.

3. Matthew 8:23-27—when I am of "little faith" or no faith and scared to death.

4. Mark 5:14-17—because Jesus understands me. Even he had people who didn't want him around.

5. Matthew 9:9-13—when I'm as loved as a tax collector!

6. Mark 5:40; Matthew 9:24—when I'm laughed at. Jesus gets that one too!

7. Matthew 9:34—when others falsely accuse me. Enemies made sure Jesus didn't belong to them and theirs.

8. Matthew 10:40—when I need a cup of cold water. Fellow believers can see I belong to Christ, and they love me just because he loves me!

9. Matthew 13:53-58; John 7:3-5—even if I'm not welcome at home. Jesus endured dishonor from friends, neighbors, and in his own home with family.

JOURNAL YOUR THOUGHTS

DAYS 85–91

Pray

Readings:

DAY 85	Matthew 14	**DAY 89**	Matthew 15
DAY 86	Mark 6	**DAY 90**	Mark 7
DAY 87	Luke 9:1-17	**DAY 91**	Matthew 16
DAY 88	John 6		

FROM MY JOURNAL

- I examine every facet of the feeding of the five thousand. The disciples were tested and got a D+ in faith. Even a trusting person can see obstacles here. At least they obeyed and handed out the food he had blessed. Imagine over five thousand dinner guests showing up and they need healing, compassion, and all-you-can-eat fish sandwiches with 12 baskets full of leftovers! I am convinced that Jesus can make much from a little. I've trusted him to do that for my family for 67 years. I've never begged for bread. I've been close a couple of times, but he always pulled me back from the brink of total loss.

- Jesus is the Bread of Life! He feeds our faith. All who are part of this feast will live forever. Jesus also walked on water and allowed Peter with his "little faith" to join him. Peter is the only one who stepped out of the boat. I'd love to trust like Peter.

- Jesus healed a deaf and mute person. Using the senses that the man still possessed, Christ identified himself as the miracle worker. Crazy, but I wondered, "Did the person he healed hear the *tha* when Jesus said, 'Be opened; Ephphatha!?'" Cool!

- The "yeast of the Pharisees and Sadducees" (Matthew 16:6) refers to the teachings of those sects. Both groups were hypocritical, overly judgmental, and based their faith on the false hope that they could save themselves.

- Poor Peter. He walked on water, declared Jesus as the Savior of the world, and then tried to talk him out of going to the cross to save us! I'm more like Peter than I know. I'm sure of it. Forgive those who spiritually fall all over themselves!

JOURNAL YOUR THOUGHTS

DAYS 92–98

Pray

Readings:

DAY 92	Mark 8	**DAY 96**	Luke 9:28-62
DAY 93	Luke 9:18-27	**DAY 97**	Matthew 18
DAY 94	Matthew 17	**DAY 98**	John 7
DAY 95	Mark 9		

FROM MY JOURNAL

- Some gospel writers recall events in chronological order (incident by incident, one day after another), while others write topically (loosely lumping accounts together as a certain subject is discussed). I also noticed an overlap from one week's readings to the next. Sometimes Jesus asked those he healed to be quiet about the miracle they received. Only among his close disciples did he allow himself to be identified as the Messiah, the chosen and anointed Savior. Jesus never wanted his ministry to become a sideshow. He taught the people so that they would believe in him because of his words.
- Christianity means a cross for believers. Only Jesus died for sin and won forgiveness on an actual cross. My cross includes the suffering I endure because I belong to him.
- Jesus revealed his true glory as the Son of God on the Mount of Transfiguration. A few disciples got a taste of heaven before seeing

hell's fury on the day Jesus died. Christ knew the cross was coming. He prepared his disciples. My 180 prepares me for what I must soon face. Get me ready, Lord!
- I never want to cause a child or a child in the faith to lose trust in Jesus. I am certain I have earned a millstone or two in my time—times when my words were right but my actions were wrong. I trust Jesus to fix this just as I am certain he wore a necklace of millstones on the day he endured the depths of hell for me. This changes me: I forgive because I am forgiven.
- John was the last gospel to be written. He does not repeat everything revealed in the first three gospels. John, however, adds to my experience as he quotes Jesus' conversations as he taught. All gospel writers were moved by the Holy Spirit to share exactly what I need to know.

JOURNAL YOUR THOUGHTS

DAYS 99–105

Pray

Readings:

DAY 99	John 8	**DAY 103**	John 10:22-42
DAY 100	John 9	**DAY 104**	Luke 12
DAY 101	John 10:1-21	**DAY 105**	Luke 13
DAY 102	Luke 10		

FROM MY JOURNAL

- Arguments over what belongs in the Bible do not need to alarm me. The vast majority of Bible verses are confirmed by ancient Greek and Hebrew texts. But some are different. Why did experts include John 7:53–8:11 in my NIV translation? A case can be made to include it. I believe it belongs. It teaches a truth Jesus demonstrated many times: drop the hypocrisy and learn to forgive. That is a good lesson for me!

- Jesus revealed himself as the great "I AM" of Moses' encounter at the burning bush. Jesus is true God. His enemies rejected that he is the Light of the world, the one who gives eternal life. I hope his enemies changed their minds about Jesus. Unbelief cannot see the miraculous or enjoy the comfort of the Good Shepherd.
- Many rejected Jesus as he taught that he was who he claimed to be: God. They baited him into arguments and tried to trap him in his words. I reread John 10:36-42. I believe the miracles and that they prove that Jesus is God's Son, that he is one with the heavenly Father.
- I am protected by a God who has the very hairs on my head all numbered. At this point in my life, there are a lot less hairs to track. Yet he knows the exact number stuck in my brush! What I pluck out and wash down the drain, he tallies to demonstrate the close watch he keeps on me. I belong to him!

JOURNAL YOUR THOUGHTS

We are over halfway to the finish. By this time in my 180, praying, reading, and journaling were part of my routine. They were as welcome as morning coffee and enjoyed like a hug from my grandchildren. God grant you the same!

A Journey With Miraculous Expectations

God promises that he can "do immeasurably more than *all* we ask or imagine" (Ephesians 3:20, emphasis added). You know, I can imagine pretty big! And here God says he is waiting to do even more than that. But should I be going so far that I'm asking for miracles? I know a Roman centurion who did. And I know a mother who just wanted crumbs for her troubled daughter. They were trusting more when they asked for the miraculous. Jesus praised that kind of faith! Remember them from chapter 3?

Try this for yourself: Think of a time you needed something you considered impossible, asked God for it, and he delivered it right into your life. Let's see. What is the first miracle I can remember asking from my God? It is one of the few early childhood recollections I have. I had to be all of three years old. I was playing with toys, but I couldn't find the one I really wanted. I searched, as much as a three-year-old searches for anything, and when I didn't find my heart's desire, I got upset. My mom did not come to the rescue. She did not come at all. I always prayed at mealtime, so I decided to ask Jesus for something now. I prayed the most awful, rebellious request ever to come out of a child's mouth: "If you are real, Jesus, give me my toy!" I turned my head and there it was, right at my side where it had been the whole time. Silly, huh? Why do I remember that? I believe Jesus was making a point to me. Even when I sat on the floor playing, he was there listening. Even when I didn't ask in the nicest, most patient way (remember, I was only three), he still lovingly and graciously gave me what I needed. He was there and ready to help if I didn't ask and when I did.

Over the years, I had many requests for what seemed miraculous: to actually make the roster of a sports team, to not live in fear like some animal in the jungle, to experience acceptance while getting used to rejection, to have a girlfriend or maybe even a wife and family someday, to be useful to Jesus (that wasn't always a given for me), to really help the people I love, and to help all those the Savior loves.

I asked for miracles many times for lots of different people. But I especially remember a time when I received a tearful phone call from my younger sister. After she helped to raise two stepchildren, she was blessed to raise two more—her sons. On this day, she was calling to share with me that she had breast cancer and that it had invaded her lymph system. The technicalities of all this bounced around in my head, but her concern cut straight to my heart. She wasn't done yet. She needed more time to raise her boys. She needed more time.

I reached for my Bible and stumbled around before finding 2 Kings 20:1-11. King Hezekiah wasn't done yet when he got his bad news. Isaiah told him, "This is what the LORD says: Put your house in order, because you are going to die; you will not recover" (2 Kings 20:1). A doctor may tell me I have stage 4 cancer. The doctor may also be wrong. The tests may show a false positive. The X-rays may have been messed up by a tech's mistake. But when God says, "Make a will; you'll soon be needing it," I better call a lawyer!

That is how King Hezekiah figured it. He turned his face to the wall, weeping as he attempted a prayer. God heard the words of the stammering king and understood the sobs. God chose to reverse his action to benefit this man. God said Hezekiah wasn't done yet. God granted him 15 more years to do his work, and important work it was. A son was born to him three years after the miraculous cure. That son, Manasseh, was his heir to the throne and through him, God continued the bloodline of kings so that God's promise would be fulfilled. The King of kings came from that royal line and now reigns forever!

My sister Kathy and I prayed Hezekiah's prayer many times after that day. We prayed it through surgery, chemo, radiation, more chemo, remission, out of remission, and during a stem cell transplant. She lived for 17 years after her initial diagnosis!

I recall some suggesting she never got her miracle. Isn't that sad? They just couldn't see, could they? God granted my sister two more years than he gave King Hezekiah! She raised her sons and repeatedly went back to the preschool room where she taught. She shared with inquisitive four-year-olds why she had lost her hair and why it grew back. And why they would need to wait for heaven to see her again. And through faith in Jesus, after she closed her eyes at the end of her earthly life, she opened them immediately to see eternal life! Don't sell it short. That too is a miracle of grace!

TIPS ALONG THE WAY

- **Find a way to remember how God answers your prayers.** I keep a record of answered prayers. I did it in my journal, but most of the time I did it in the pages of my mind. It is amazing how attentive God has been to me! My family has recognized this and has suggested I have a special "hotline" to the Almighty. I guess I do, but that connection is the same one we all have, and his name is Jesus. He is our unlimited access to our heavenly Father. I use that connection; I "ask," "seek," and "knock" (Matthew 7:7), and God answers in the way that is best.

- **Trust God's answer to your prayers.** In college, I worked at a nursing home. The business manager was a fine Christian man, and he and his wife prayed for a child. They received a little baby girl who was extremely ill. The manager quoted Jesus' promise: "I will do whatever you ask in my name. . . . You may ask me for anything in my name, and I will do it" (John 14:13-14). He asked for healing, for a normal life for his daughter. I cautioned him to pray in Jesus' name, which means according to Jesus' plan and in accord with Jesus' all-knowing will. His daughter died as a baptized child of God. Now, I can argue with God's decision, but in the end, I have no doubt he is right. Jesus did not fail that little girl. He did the wisest thing for her. Jesus gave her a perfect life that will last forever instead of only a temporary life for the here and now.

- **Trusting more means praying big.** I need miracles every time I need help from the Lord. That is how I see it. When I hit the wall, when frustration makes me throw up my hands in surrender, when in fear and worry I tremble and beg, I am asking for divine intervention that God alone can give me to help me get past a problem or to learn how to live with it. When I think about it, it's a miracle either way.

◊ **Trusting more means praying humbly.** I don't demand miracles. I don't claim them as if God owes them to me. I don't test God with an "or else" like I did when I was three. I know God is not only smarter than I am, but he is also on a whole different plane of understanding. Look at Isaiah 55:9. I do not have his eyes to see the future. I do not perceive how one event collides with another to bless thousands. I do not have the wisdom of the ages or the power of creation. Most of the time, I am limited to seeing how something affects me. I don't take time to consider how it affects everyone else. I need to give God's will, plan, and intentions room to work. Even if he answers my prayer with a no, I trust he has something better in mind. A Christian friend once taught me this: "God will not give you what is good when he plans to give you the best!"

Trusting more, I humbly ask my God for miracles. I confess to him that I have no right to ask for them, but I am coming to him anyway. I bring Jesus with me, and as the Father greets his Son, he sees me as his adopted child through faith. I ask for what is beyond my power to do. And boy, is that a list! I give it to God for an answer, believing he has heard me and that whatever he does, even before I see it happening, deserves my thanks.

DAYS 106–112

Pray

Readings:

DAY 106 Luke 14	**DAY 110** John 11
DAY 107 Luke 15	**DAY 111** Luke 17:11-37
DAY 108 Luke 16	**DAY 112** Luke 18:1-14
DAY 109 Luke 17:1-10	

FROM MY JOURNAL

- Jesus heals and teaches, admonishing pride. The Savior loves humility and despises arrogance. Humble faith hears and obeys Jesus' invitation to the banquet of salvation. Humble believers hear Christ's call to bear the cross for his sake.

- In parables, Jesus tells me the great value he places on a single soul. He encourages me to use my worldly resources to make heavenly friends. After this life, money will be meaningless. True treasure is found in "Moses and the Prophets" (Luke 16:29), a reference to God's entire Word.

- Jesus has the power to raise a decomposing corpse from the dead and restore the person to the picture of health. We have seen him heal disease and raise others from the dead. He can do anything! Miracles? No problem for him!

- Leprosy is a slow death. Ten lepers. Ten healings. But little thanks. If I am too busy to see a miracle, why would I thank Jesus? If I explain miracles away, why would I express gratitude? The Samaritan saw that he was miraculously healed and came back to give thanks to the healer. A lack of thankfulness does not negate the healing, but after a miracle, my faith needs to say, "Thank you!"

- Jesus wants me to pester him with my persistent prayers. Faith will not give up. My Lord asks me to be humble in repentance and as confident as a child in his love and mercy.

JOURNAL YOUR THOUGHTS

DAYS 113–119

Pray

Readings:

DAY 113 Matthew 19
DAY 114 Mark 10
DAY 115 Matthew 20
DAY 116 Matthew 21
DAY 117 Luke 18:15-43
DAY 118 Luke 19
DAY 119 Mark 11

FROM MY JOURNAL

- Jesus loves marriage and family. And it is his will that I protect it. Trusting more means fighting for my family members, not with them.
- Blind Bartimaeus and an unnamed friend received mercy and restored eyes to see the Savior. I have never been physically blind, but I have been spiritually blind. I can only have the inheritance of heaven by trusting in Christ. Trusting more, I see it is impossible for earthly riches or anything else to save me. Trust God, who does the impossible and saves us through his Son. I "was blind but now I see" (CW 576), thanks to God's mercy.
- Jesus predicted his death. He publicly rode past waving palm branches toward the cross. Prophecy was fulfilled. Faith and hypocrisy huddled in the street to receive the King. Murderous plots thickened. Constant attacks were repelled by insightful, biblical teaching. I am amazed at Jesus' patience with his enemies! He

- taught them in order to make inroads into their hearts—a king who overcomes enemies and, at the same time, works to save them.
- In the parable of the ten minas, Jesus warns of a day of reckoning and reward. He has given me health, wealth, education, family, friends, freedom, his Word, and a heart of faith in the gift of the Savior. I am called to invest all of it to produce dividends that give him glory. I admit that I'm not always a good manager of such great wealth. I confess that sometimes I misuse it. Forgive your servant, Lord, and I would gladly respond like Zacchaeus (Luke 19:8)!

JOURNAL YOUR THOUGHTS

DAYS 120–126

Pray

Readings:

DAY 120	John 12	DAY 124	Luke 20
DAY 121	Matthew 22	DAY 125	Luke 21
DAY 122	Mark 12	DAY 126	Mark 13
DAY 123	Matthew 23

FROM MY JOURNAL

- Judas, the critic and thief, objected to a beautiful offering of faith. As the fragrance of expensive perfume fills the air, I learn that extravagance has its place in worshiping Jesus. As I write this, my church is in the middle of a building project. I want the structure, furnishings, and equipment to demonstrate our collective love for Christ. Think for a moment, how much did the widow give to God? Just two cents? Just *everything!*
- Jesus' enemies wanted to kill Lazarus, the same man raised from death and decay. How far will unbelief go to destroy evidence of miracles? Hard hearts do monstrous things! Jesus would be lifted

on a cross and would give his Father glory as sin and unbelief murdered him.
- Already in Luke, Mark, and next week in Matthew, judgment day is mentioned. This earth will end. And Jesus will return to take us to his heavenly kingdom. I'm alert and watching, but I'm not afraid of that day. I know the judge who holds court. He has nail marks in his hands!

JOURNAL YOUR THOUGHTS

DAYS 127–133

Pray

Readings:

DAY 127	Matthew 24	**DAY 131**	Luke 22
DAY 128	Matthew 25	**DAY 132**	John 13
DAY 129	Matthew 26	**DAY 133**	John 14
DAY 130	Mark 14		

FROM MY JOURNAL

- Do I live *for* Jesus or *not for* Jesus? Yes. I've seen Christ in the truly needy. I have helped. But I have also turned away. My kind or unkind actions will not save me when the King comes to separate the sheep (believers) from the goats (unbelievers) (Matthew 25:31-46). By God's grace I am a sheep who hears my Shepherd's voice and knows he died defending the flock. Just a dumb, helpless sheep. I need my Shepherd-King to save me. My acts of love for Jesus are evidence that he has saved me and that I belong to him.
- Jesus taught with words and by example. Scrubbing dirty feet isn't half as nauseating as cleansing my filthy soul. Washed by the Savior, I am comforted with thoughts of my heavenly home. Jesus, the

carpenter's son, built and prepared it for me with his death and resurrection. The Lord gives me his Spirit and his peace. Because of this, I am not troubled or afraid.

- Judas betrayed, Peter denied, disciples fled to escape, and Jesus was arrested and convicted in a crooked court. There was no evidence to condemn him. He would die because he told the truth. Under oath, he revealed he is the Messiah (the promised Savior) and the Son of God. He had the power to stop this miscarriage of justice. He wouldn't because I need him to finish the plan that rescues me forever.

- Jesus gave his family of faith the Lord's Supper. Disciples ate bread and drank wine and received what Jesus promised: "my body" and "my blood," "*given* for you" and "*poured out* for you" (Luke 22:19-20, emphasis added). At Communion, I am at the cross. This is the real thing! I don't pass up an opportunity to go to this meal. Jesus is there assuring me and each believer, "I gave my body and blood *for you!*" A miracle right before my eyes!

JOURNAL YOUR THOUGHTS

Still with me? Trust in God is itself a miracle powered by the Holy Spirit through God's Word. It is a miracle God put us on this 180 journey because we want to trust him even more. And with his help, we'll finish it!

Destination Ahead: Trusting Through Life's End

Death is not natural. Ever since the movie *The Lion King*, and maybe even since before that, the idea has become more common and more popular that death is simply a natural part of every creature's life cycle, a part that is simply supposed to be there. There is a circle of life because of the fall of the human race, but it wasn't supposed to be this way. God's original intent was for me to stroll through the perfect garden he created, walk up to the tree of life, harvest its fruit, and live forever. Sin's contamination changed all that. Now my life cycle is like an apple out of my orchard: it starts as a blossom (young and beautiful); then it becomes a bud (full of promise); suddenly it is green and growing (my potential is realized); then ripe (my life in its full glory); then overripe (as I begin to realize I'm losing my former vitality and my body is breaking down); until finally it is mush ready for the compost pile (the end of life).

Jesus makes all that different. God's Son died to settle my sin debt, but he rose again so that death itself would die. Through faith in Jesus, my life will not end. I will "not perish but have eternal life" (John 3:16). And Jesus promised, "The one who believes in me will live, even though they die; and whoever lives by believing in me will never die" (John 11:25-26). Should you ever visit the cemetery where my lifeless body will be kept for the day of resurrection, you will know where I rest. I want no dates, no name, and no pledge that I will be missed. On my gravestone let it read: "NEVER DIE—John 11:25."

The moment of death doesn't bother me. I'll be struggling down the path through the "valley of the shadow of death" (Psalm 23:4 Evangelical Heritage Version), and Jesus will appear just as he promises. I'll say, "Lord, I've been looking for you!" And he'll say, "I've always been right here beside you." Together we will approach the door to his Father's house, where he has promised he is preparing a place for me (John 14:1-6). And because of Jesus, I will see that door open.

My problem is what is leading up to the valley. Death is no sweat, but dying, oh my! As a boy, I always imagined I'd die during a persecution of Christianity. I thought I would be staring down lions just before lunch . . . their lunch! As I got older, I'd bargain with God on deaths I'd prefer and those I'd like to be spared: no drowning (which almost happened once), no burning to death (which also almost happened once—someday I'll tell you the story), and nothing with torture. That left God with plenty of room to work with for my escape from this planet. Oh yes, and I didn't want to die a prolonged death . . . like my mother.

Bone cancer took three years to claim my mother. Slowly, she inched toward heaven. Each morning she'd ask, "Am I still here?" She would wince in pain and add, "Why doesn't God just let me die?"

On an especially bad afternoon, I was sitting next to her and holding her hand. She looked at me, asking, "Why am I here?"

I said, "Because I need you."

She said, "Oh no, let me go!"

I said, "In God's time, but for now I need you to do me a favor. You have taught me almost everything I needed to know in life except one thing."

She grew interested: "What is it, dear?"

I said, "Teach me how a Christian faces death."

You know, that helped her. She had a godly purpose for her suffering. Each time I'd sit at her side, she'd give me a play-by-play of wha she was going through, her sorrows and her joys, and she always shared a steady confidence that she trusted Jesus to keep his Word. I remember her saying, "When I die, don't cry for me. Jesus will take me home, and I long to go home!" Amen!

On the day she was buried, I served as a pallbearer along with my brothers (one by birth and one by law) and her brothers. As we left the church and began sliding the coffin into the hearse, I laid my hand on the lid and said with dry eyes, "I'll see you again very soon!"

Soon. As I look forward to that day, I pause and wonder. There's a lot I don't know. Will a lot of people attend my funeral? It doesn't matter. Will I look good resting in that box? I don't look good now! Can a funeral director make me look like a young Robert Redford? That would be nice! But there is one thing I know. I won't be there should you attend. I'll be living out my eternity with Jesus and all who love him. And when we meet in the resurrection, I'll be pleased to introduce you to my mom!

TIPS ALONG THE WAY

- **Trusting God more helps you deal with fears about death.** I'm not a morbid guy, but I do think about death and dying. If the same is true for you, don't run from these thoughts and don't hide from the inevitable. Instead, consider the wonderful things Jesus promises believers in the new life of heaven. Do you ever get night sweats when you wake with thoughts of the grave burying you? In those moments, I pray, "Jesus, you are the Resurrection and the Life. I can't outdistance the grave, so you must free me from it. I cannot beat death, but you did. And you promise you will give me the same victory. I trust you to get me through this, just as I trust you to calm me down and get me back to sleep. Amen!"

- **Trusting God more helps you get ready to face your own death.** My 180 had me asking if my house is in order. I'm not dying any more or any less than you are, but I talked to my wife about what I want for a funeral. She knows my favorite hymns: it will be a Christmas and Easter event with old gospel numbers on the side. I checked about life insurance. I have a burial policy. I will soon have an updated will. I'm good with cremation, but remember to consider your family's wishes as you prepare your final wishes. Remember, your soul will be safe in heaven with Jesus. It is your family and friends still living here who will need the comfort. So if even one of my family members needs a viewing and full body burial, I'm also happy to let my body rest in the box.

- **Trusting God more helps you prepare others for when you go home to heaven.** My funeral will praise Jesus for his amazing grace and thank him for his gift of heaven—it is my home. I've asked a young man from my Sunday school class to comfort my family at the funeral. He has agreed. He is the herald who will announce, "My teacher believed Jesus died for him and gave him heaven!" I will find a way to pay for the tuition for that young man to become a pastor should he hear

God's call. Estate planning! I thought about what I want to say to my children and grandchildren as they gather around my deathbed. Rather than commit all that to memory, I decided to start talking to them now! I tell them how much I love them while I can still show them. I give away keepsakes and tell them to remember they are from Dad or Grandpa. I don't need the stuff, and they get such enjoyment out of it. I tell them I am proud of them, and I follow up by telling them why. God has blessed me through them; I'm pleased they are mine.

DAYS 134–140

Pray

Readings:

DAY 134	John 15	DAY 138	Mark 15
DAY 135	John 16	DAY 139	Luke 23
DAY 136	John 17	DAY 140	John 18
DAY 137	Matthew 27		

FROM MY JOURNAL

- It was still dinner conversation on the night before Jesus would die. There was a lot that still needed to be said. Jesus is my vine and I'm alive in faith through my connection to him. If it's good in my life, it is from him. So I make my floundering attempts to sincerely love because I am loved by him. The sinful world hates Jesus and will hate any Christian who stands up for him. I have felt that hate. Christ's love has more than made up for it.

- A mother gives birth knowing in a little while her pain and grief will turn to pure joy as her child enters life. I have the labor pains of sorrow, grief, pain, and sadness. Life is hard! Soon I will see Jesus again. He has overcome this world. I take heart and do slow breathing to get through today.

- I am reminded of a hymn when I read about Jesus' crucifixion: "Stricken, smitten, and afflicted, see him dying on the tree!" (CW 430). Mocked and tormented, Jesus keeps his loving composure. His words teach us what we need to know about death and dying:

  1. **"Father, forgive them, for they do not know what they are doing" (Luke 23:34).** When dying, I want people to know I forgive them. I won't carry grudges to the grave.

  2. **"Today you will be with me in paradise" (Luke 23:43).** I will share Jesus as the way to heaven. This may be my last

chance to tell people I love, whether they are in the faith or not, what the saved need to know.

3. **"Here is your mother" (John 19:27).** I will care for those who are watching me die. I will remind loved ones of plans that have been made for their physical well-being.

4. **"My God, my God, why have you forsaken me?" (Matthew 27:46).** Jesus was forsaken as he was punished for my sins. He was forsaken so that I will never be forsaken. God is with me even as I die.

5. **"I am thirsty" (John 19:28).** Jesus fulfills the prophecy and reminds me that I will have physical needs in the dying process. Some of those needs may have simple solutions. Ask for care and relief.

6. **"It is finished" (John 19:30).** Christ completely paid my eternal debt. My sin is gone and so my guilt is gone too. I haven't earned heaven. Jesus did it for me!

7. **"Father, into your hands I commit my spirit" (Luke 23:46).** Through faith, God is my Father and in death I'm going to him. Set aside your fears, John! It's homecoming in heaven!

- Scripture does not mandate a certain type of burial or burial service. If it did, after death I'd be wrapped in a spice-filled sheet and placed in a cave. I will ask my family before my time comes and do the loving thing. Options include full body burial or cremation; casket or urn; to be buried in a grave, a mausoleum, or out on the "back 20" if the law allows. Whether there is a viewing or no viewing, a catered lunch or coffee and cake is up to my family. But this is not optional: I want a celebration of God's grace to me with gospel words of comfort for all who mourn and need hope renewed!

JOURNAL YOUR THOUGHTS

DAYS 141–147

Pray

Readings:

DAY 141 John 19	**DAY 145** John 20
DAY 142 Matthew 28	**DAY 146** John 21
DAY 143 Mark 16	**DAY 147** Acts 1
DAY 144 Luke 24	

FROM MY JOURNAL

- I appreciate the special details that John adds to the account of Good Friday. He was the only one of the Twelve listed as being at the foot of the cross as Jesus died. Other disciples, like the women, Joseph of Arimathea, and Nicodemus, were also present for the crucifixion or Jesus' burial. In Romans 6:1-14, the apostle Paul says I was at Jesus' death and burial too. Through my baptism, I am intimately connected to Jesus' death, burial, and resurrection. The Savior died my death on the cross. Now I am as unresponsive as a corpse when it comes to sin, and I live a new life of faith for him.

- I highlighted the details of Easter. They are written for me. I believe in the physical resurrection of Jesus. He really came back from the dead. This makes me certain that his work to save me is completed. The Father did not leave him in the grave or view his effort as a failure. The risen and victorious Jesus is all the proof I need that he is God, his Word is true, and he has the power to raise me and all believers to eternal life!

- The book of Acts continues the account of the first-century Christian church. The gospel of Luke and the book of Acts were both authored by the disciple Luke and addressed to Theophilus. They were intended to be companion volumes.

- The risen Jesus ascended back to heaven. His human body is away from my eyes, but he is still with me "to the very end of the age"

(Matthew 28:20). I will see him with my own eyes when he returns on the Last Day!
- All believers are called to make disciples by baptizing in the name of the triune God and teaching all of Jesus' Word. This is called the Great Commission, but really it is my commission. Whether working a job or retired, I'm always on call to witness Christ to the world.

JOURNAL YOUR THOUGHTS

DAYS 148–154

Pray

Readings:

DAY 148 Acts 2	**DAY 152** Acts 6
DAY 149 Acts 3	**DAY 153** Acts 7
DAY 150 Acts 4	**DAY 154** Acts 8
DAY 151 Acts 5	

FROM MY JOURNAL

- Jesus said that when he finished his work, he would send the Holy Spirit to be our advocate and teacher. On Pentecost, 50 days after Easter, that promise was fulfilled. The Holy Spirit came in the sound of a great wind and gave the disciples courage to speak, good news to tell, languages to overcome barriers, and a crowd to hear the message: "Repent and be baptized, every one of you, in the name of Jesus Christ for the forgiveness of your sins. And you will receive the gift of the Holy Spirit" (Acts 2:38). I want all those gifts for my loved ones. Lord, bring all my grandchildren to Baptism for the Spirit's gifts!
- Enemies of Jesus, both inside and outside the church, tried to stop the disciples from spreading the Savior's Word. But wherever

believers are forced to flee, they carry the message of Jesus' cross and empty tomb. Am I still trusting God more if I'm ever in a situation where I feel the need to flee? If I bring the message of Jesus along with me to share with others, the answer is yes.

JOURNAL YOUR THOUGHTS

DAYS 155–161

Pray

Readings:

DAY 155	Acts 9	DAY 159	Acts 13
DAY 156	Acts 10	DAY 160	Acts 14
DAY 157	Acts 11	DAY 161	Acts 15
DAY 158	Acts 12		

FROM MY JOURNAL

- Saul, the persecutor, was called by Jesus to become Paul, the preacher and missionary. This was a real 180 for him! Peter, the orthodox Jew, was called to share Jesus with non-Jewish people. Another 180! God's grace is for everyone. I have never met anyone he doesn't love. The early church needed time to understand this. It had Peter's vision, Paul's experience, the Scriptures' witness, and a council's verdict to pave the way for a worldwide church.
- I love how believers prayed for Peter's release from prison but were surprised when he was knocking at the door! Pray, and expect the unexpected!
- Mission work is a joy as the Holy Spirit grants the Word success. I need to pray for missionaries because they must also face rejection and opposition in their work. Lord, encourage and bless them!

JOURNAL YOUR THOUGHTS

The Journey Continues

From little on to the present day, I have always been a big guy. My mother said I shouldn't be ashamed that I was husky. Once in my life, just before I was married, I reached my ideal adult weight. My relatives were certain I was wasting away and wanted me to go to a doctor to be sure I was alright. Marriage was a turning point for me. I gained 20 pounds in sympathy weight when my wife was carrying our first child. Those 20 pounds never came off. While working a desk job and without strenuous exercise, I pushed the scale ever higher.

There is an assumption about larger people. One day they just didn't care and the next day they looked like a tank. Not so with me. The process was slow, and a lifetime later the results are beyond argument. Do the math. A man is 5'10" and ideally weighs 178 pounds. Now add a yearly cycle where you gain 10 pounds each winter but take 5 pounds off with diet and exercise. That is a net gain of 5 pounds. Not so bad unless you multiply that by 36 years of more of the same. When I retired, that is exactly where I was. Having too much extra body weight is unhealthy. With my doctor's guidance and my wife's help, I have reversed the cycle by six years in three-and-a-half years of effort. At this rate, I'll be back to my ideal weight by about the time I'm 90! Isn't that something to work toward? I'll be healthier for it along the way.

When it comes to faith, many Christians have the opposite problem. Their trust was strong and big, back when they were worshiping every

Sunday or attending a parochial elementary school or high school. They were cruising in their Christianity while they were involved in campus ministry, or while the kids were in Sunday school, they went to Bible class every week. Then a cycle began. "Oh, I know enough. I believe enough. I was confirmed in the Christian faith. I was active. I attended a Christian school. I taught Bible class back then. But I'm really busy now. Faith gets the crumbs of my time. I have important things to do."

Faith slips away like pounds packed onto our frames, a little every year. Then one day, we have to face the reality of who we have become. Maybe it's when a crisis attacks where we are. Or when a family emergency shakes us down to the bottom of our souls. We ask, "What happened to me? God and I were close once. I don't know what I believe anymore. I feel forgotten. Unwelcome. Outside the family. Outside God's family."

For a number of years, I did some consulting work. After I would go through a process of self-awareness with a client, there would be a time of instruction and restructuring. And then I would help evaluate positive change. There would be an assessment of what worked and how it made life easier. Could I try that now for us?

1. Was my 180 an informative experience?

_____

_____

_____

_____

2. Was my 180 a motivational experience?

_____

_____

_____

_____

_____

3. Was I challenged by my 180 to change my way of life?

4. What, if anything, changed for the better because I took part in my 180?

5. What, if anything, changed for the worse because I took part in my 180?

6. Did my 180 become a welcomed and constructive habit for me?

_____

_____

_____

_____

_____

7. What impact will my 180 have on my future?

_____

_____

_____

_____

_____

I'll share my own evaluation. There are not many secrets between us now. I've been honest with you so far, so I won't stop now. I really enjoyed my 180. I have redeveloped the good habit of personally reading my Bible. My prayers have been more specific, with heart, mind, and mouth working together in harmony. Many days, God's Spirit had me in the right place at the right time for spiritual growth. Without my planning, God took me to a passage or promise that I needed to answer the struggle of the day. I discovered I was becoming a grumpy old man and that was inconsistent with my faith. I have become more aware of my thought processes, quick words, and careless actions. Have all the negatives disappeared? I am not in heaven yet! But I'm more aware. I have gotten more out of the readings and hymns at church. It has surprised me how those texts often match what I have been studying for the week.

My 180 is still a daily process, but don't discount this: More is more. I apologize more. I look for ways to serve more. I run to Jesus for forgiveness even more than before, often because my readings remind me of his will. I miss it if I don't read the Scriptures each day. I crave more quiet time with God, just me and my God. My 180 will continue. I've been a believer from infancy, but of this idea I am even more convinced: Either I am growing in faith through God's Word, or I am losing faith. Body weight? That can diminish. Trust in God? I want more and more. I pray this is your experience too!

TIPS ALONG THE WAY

- **Continue to build on this spiritually healthy habit you've developed.** I plan to continue my Bible reading right where I left off. I still can pray, read, journal, and ask my "W's." I'll need a new notebook and another highlighter and I'm ready to go!

- **Even if you are rereading a familiar section of the Bible, try to take away something new each time.** I can go back in another year and ask a different question about the same readings I just finished. Try it. Reread the gospels, only this time, ask: "What, in these verses, does God say to me about my marriage?" or "What does God reveal that my children need in their teen years?" or "What does this say to me as a citizen of my country?"

- **Try another book in the series!** Need additional help? The My 180 series helps you navigate your storms.

As we sprint to the finish of your 180, we will read some of Paul's letters in their entirety. I have selected several that I read, each in a single sitting. It is doable. Don't neglect to read the introduction to each letter if you have one included in your Bible. It will remind you of details you have already learned on the missionary trail in Acts.

DAYS 162–168

Pray

Readings:

DAY 162	Acts 16	**DAY 166**	Acts 20
DAY 163	Acts 17	**DAY 167**	Acts 21
DAY 164	Acts 18	**DAY 168**	Acts 22
DAY 165	Acts 19		

FROM MY JOURNAL

- God plans how his church will expand. Acts 16:6-10 reminds me that I need God's blessing on my planning and my timetable. I walk through life and God directs the work. He determines where the gospel is spread. Case in point, I met two prospective believers at the gym this morning! And I just went there to exercise.

- Persecution always pursues the message of Christ. I shouldn't be surprised or alarmed. Put me in stocks and lock me in prison, and God will make a way for his will to be done.

- Enjoy allies of the gospel. We are blessed when we recognize others in the faith. Is their Christian understanding the same as mine? Some know more and are sent to teach me. Others know less and I am there to teach them. Where would Apollos have been without Priscilla and Aquila?

- Jesus' disciples became known as apostles because they were sent out to proclaim Christ to the nations. God did miracles through them to convince crowds that his power is with their words. Acts 20:7-12 is one of my favorite accounts. A tired young man, a long sermon, a terrible accident: all combined for a resurrection miracle!

JOURNAL YOUR THOUGHTS

DAYS 169–175

Pray

Readings:

DAY 169	Acts 23	DAY 173	Acts 27
DAY 170	Acts 24	DAY 174	Acts 28
DAY 171	Acts 25	DAY 175	Galatians
DAY 172	Acts 26		

FROM MY JOURNAL

- Paul confused his enemies and ended up in protective custody. His work in Jerusalem was done. It was God's time to send Paul to Rome. Some plotted the apostle's murder, but God prevented it from happening. At each turn in the road, through long days in court, delays, and an appeal to Caesar, Paul confessed Jesus. What seems like trouble to me may prove an open door for Christ.

- People began calling Christianity "the way." And "the way" was on its way to Rome. Paul was on a voyage that left him shipwrecked and snakebit but ultimately at his destination. Even under house arrest, Paul told his guards about their Savior. Amazing! Christianity is unstoppable! Blessed by the risen Lord!

- I read Paul's letter to the Galatians. I can add nothing to Jesus' work for my salvation. Works, obedience, circumcision, or no circumcision—nothing saves me but Christ alone! Why should God let me into heaven? If my answer somehow points to my accomplishments, I am lost forever. My plea: "Jesus. Just Jesus!"

JOURNAL YOUR THOUGHTS

DAYS 176–180 AND BEYOND!

Pray

Readings:

DAY 176 Ephesians	**DAY 179** Romans 1–4
DAY 177 Philippians	**DAY 180** Romans 5–8
DAY 178 Colossians	

FROM MY JOURNAL

- Pray. Try hard to find a theme or reason for each letter as you read it completely through. Mark memorable passages. Journal and answer your "W's." Enjoy it. This is not homework. It is time with God.
- **Ephesians:** God has chosen me in his grace. He has raised me from death in sin to life in Christ. I live as someone resurrected, battling temptation with the armor of God.
- **Philippians:** Paul waited for his death in prison. If he died, Jesus would take him to heaven. If he lived, he would work for Christ. I am led to be humble in suffering, following my Lord's example, and led to be content in all things. I have Jesus. I can deal with anything!
- **Colossians:** I shouldn't chase every religious fad, seer of visions, revealer of mysteries, or teacher of the latest wisdom. I have Christ and his Word. It is all I need. Loving my Savior, my life is his!
- **Romans:** Whether we are wildly living in sin, judgmental and thinking ourselves better than others, or earnest in trying to keep all the commandments to save ourselves, we are all in the same boat! We are equally lost and are only right in God's sight through faith in our Savior Jesus Christ. "God demonstrates his own love for us in this: While we were still sinners, Christ died for us" (Romans 5:8). Because we are God's chosen children, all of life must work for our benefit. God has us on the path to heaven. How bad can life ever really be?

JOURNAL YOUR THOUGHTS

DAY 181

Why stop? The rest of the Bible is waiting for you! Grow in faith and trust God more!